HOW TO SU

CW00542345

MEDIŁ vAL
ENGLAND

For Elliot Samuel Mount
The youngest member of the family
And so the most likely to have the chance to become a time-traveller

HOW TO SURVIVE IN MEDIEVAL ENGLAND

TONI MOUNT

PEN & SWORD
HISTORY

AN IMPRINT OF PEN & SWORD BOOKS LTD.
YORKSHIRE - PHILADELPHIA

First published in Great Britain in 2021 by
PEN AND SWORD HISTORY
An imprint of
Pen & Sword Books Ltd
Yorkshire – Philadelphia

Copyright © Toni Mount, 2021

ISBN 978 1 52675 441 7

The right of Toni Mount to be identified as Author of
this work has been asserted by him in accordance with the Copyright,
Designs and Patents Act 1988.

A CIP catalogue record for this book is available from the British Library.

All rights reserved. No part of this book may be reproduced or transmitted in
any form or by any means, electronic or mechanical including photocopying,
recording or by any information storage and retrieval system, without permission
from the Publisher in writing.

Typeset in Times New Roman 11.5/14 by
SJmagic DESIGN SERVICES, India.
Printed and bound by CPI Group (UK) Ltd, Croydon CR0 4YY

Pen & Sword Books Limited incorporates the imprints of Atlas, Archaeology,
Aviation, Discovery, Family History, Fiction, History, Maritime, Military,
Military Classics, Politics, Select, Transport, True Crime, Air World,
Frontline Publishing, Leo Cooper, Remember When, Seaforth Publishing,
The Praetorian Press, Wharncliffe Local History, Wharncliffe Transport,
Wharncliffe True Crime and White Owl.

For a complete list of Pen & Sword titles please contact
PEN & SWORD BOOKS LIMITED
47 Church Street, Barnsley, South Yorkshire, S70 2AS, England
E-mail: enquiries@pen-and-sword.co.uk
Website: www.pen-and-sword.co.uk

Or

PEN AND SWORD BOOKS
1950 Lawrence Rd, Havertown, PA 19083, USA
E-mail: Uspen-and-sword@casematepublishers.com
Website: www.penandswordbooks.com

Contents

Chapter 1

Introduction

It may happen in my grandchildren's lifetimes, or those of their grandchildren, that mankind will learn the secrets of time-travel and Doctor Who's TARDIS becomes a reality. I have no idea what twenty-second century technology will be like. Perhaps books such as this won't exist and 'readers' will simply choose a title, connect to it in some way, through the ether, and the entire text will be implanted into their minds for future reference. Personally, I prefer turning pages.

However mysterious our future may be, at least we know something about our past. This book is intended as a handy guide to the dos and don'ts for visitors to Medieval England: do be polite, don't drink the water, do wear rabbit fur, don't expect to eat with a fork, etc. How do you find your way around without GPS, Sat Nav or even signposts? Where can you get a decent meal; what will be served and how will it taste? What should you do if you meet royalty? If you're not well, who should you see about it? Where can you stay? What should you wear for a night on the town? How do you contact a friend or relative[1] without social media or skype and no wi-fi to look up information? (For looking stuff up, I'm afraid this book is all that will be available.) And most importantly, how do you get money to spend when there are no credit/debit cards or cash points, or even banks?

You won't have any relatives: they haven't been born yet, but you will definitely have living ancestors, if you can identify them.[1]

You'll find the answers to these questions and many more here, produced in a user-friendly format you can take with you on your travels back to the Middle Ages (unless you downloaded it on Kindle, in which case, it's only of use for as long as the battery remains charged).

Setting the Scene

Labourers working in fields.

Medieval England is an agricultural land. Depending upon the date of your visit, the scenery may be rather different. Back in 1066, when William the Conqueror defeated the last Anglo-Saxon king, Harold II, at the battle of Hastings, he found England a prosperous country – the main reason he was so keen to become its king – dotted with few towns but many villages and hamlets, each with its own three-field system, growing crops in rotation. This means the arable land is divided into three fields: one growing wheat, barley, oats or rye, depending on the soil type and local climate; one sown with peas and beans, which restore nutrients to the soil; and the third left fallow, to be grazed by livestock to add their manure to the earth. Each year the use of the field rotates, keeping them all fertile, and they are divided into strips, owned by each villager in such a way that everyone has a share of the best land and the poorest. Most houses come with a garden plot, where the household grows onions, cabbages, leeks and herbs. Every village has its common land, where the locals graze their animals, and often an orchard with apple, pear, plum and cherry trees. Here the beehives, or skeps, are kept, to ensure the bees pollinate the blossom to give a good harvest of fruit and to produce honey; the poor man's only sweetener. The village probably has areas of woodland as well, which supply timber for building, kindling for the fire, free nuts and berries in the autumn and 'pannage' for pigs.

DID YOU KNOW?

The 'right of pannage' gives legal permission to locals to let their pigs roam the woods, feasting on acorns and beechnuts (mast), to fatten the animals for the November slaughter.

plough, sow, weed and harvest. Houses left empty when the occupants died could be pillaged to improve those still inhabited, and the poorer hovels of the remaining villagers could now be exchanged for more affluent dwellings, with the result that landlords were eager for the receipt of higher rents for better accommodation.

The lords' incomes had reduced greatly with the loss of rents from so many empty tenancies and yet the labourers were demanding better pay. The aristocracy brought in new laws in an attempt to prevent the lower classes from rising above their God-ordained humble status, but in the long run the common folk had generally improved their lot by the early fifteenth-century.

The lords found a way of making good their lost revenues by enclosing fields that had once grown crops as pasture for thousands of sheep. Labour costs were reduced to the wages of a few shepherds with extra hands at shearing time, and the profits from wool exports more than made up for the loss of rental income. All was well until the population began to increase again in the sixteenth century and greedy lords gave over too much land to sheep farming and not enough to food production. Unemployment and hunger among the lower classes resulted, but we need not worry about that since our time parameters are 1154-1485: the era of the Plantagenet kings of England.

Apart from the changes in landscape, as travellers you need to consider the means of getting around. Roads are a bit of a problem throughout the period. The best and most direct routes between larger towns and cities are often the ruinous remains of the Roman roads, laid down a millennium before. For much of the route taken by Geoffrey Chaucer's pilgrims from London to Canterbury, they were following the old Roman Watling Street. If you journey from London to York via Lincoln, on the Great North Road, you will in fact be using much the same route as the Roman legions who marched along Ermine Street. These roads may be pot-holed and subsiding in places, or worn away to muddy tracks, but they will be busy with foot traffic, laden carts and horses, so you shouldn't get lost. However, there are no signposts or proper maps, so if your journey takes you to some lesser-known village you will need a guide or be prepared to ask directions. Be aware, however: the locals are likely to be suspicious of strangers and may not give you a truthful answer.

Wherever you travel, it's best to go with company – as Chaucer's pilgrims did – because there is always the danger of attack by bandits, robbers and ne'er-do-wells. The law states that trees and bushes should be kept cut back for a hundred yards on either side of the road, so such malefactors can't hide in ambush for unwary travellers. But that requires a great deal of time and work and is rarely done. You may want to arm yourself with a stout stave; this will not only aid your walking, but in an emergency can help you pole-vault over puddles, test the depth of water as you cross streams or serve as a weapon, if you are unfortunate enough to be accosted by robbers.

Top Tip

Always keep your purse hidden out of sight under your clothes. Medieval thieves are known as 'cut-purses' for a reason. But at least there are no pickpockets as pockets haven't been invented yet.

At the end of the day, you'll want somewhere to sleep and get a meal. If you find an abbey or a smaller priory, the monks or nuns are obliged to give you bed and board for one night. (Board refers to the trestle boards used as tables, so it means that you get food.) In theory their hospitality is free, but, in fact, they will expect you to make a donation or small gift to the religious house. It is wise to do so, especially if you intend to stay there again on your return journey, because monks and nuns have long memories for such things. If you can't afford to pay, you could be expected to do a day's labour instead: mucking out the cowshed, reaping in the hay meadow or helping with the laundry. Only those going about God's own business, such as priests, friars, visiting monks or lay people on pilgrimage, truly get their hospitality free.

Be warned: in the guesthouse you may have to share a bed with a complete stranger or two, along with fleas, bed bugs, lice, etc. Also, the food may not be to your taste. These things apply, even if you stay in a proper roadside inn. It may be a wise precaution to carry a bottle of lavender water to use as an insect repellent. Since we know – as folk at the time didn't – that plague is transmitted by fleas, I think this is essential and could be a life-saver.

Your fellow travellers may not worry about verminous insects but they are concerned about the food they'll be served. It is, therefore, expected that you will carry a small flask or bottle of what might be termed 'vinaigrette', a mixture of your favourite seasonings such as vinegar, mustard seed, salt, a few herbs, garlic and perhaps pepper and olive oil, if you can afford such luxuries.

The idea is that you use this mixture to improve – or disguise – the flavour of the food you are served. Since vinegar, garlic and herbs, such as sage, have antiseptic and antibiotic properties, your vinaigrette can also fight the bacteria present in poorly prepared food. Though nobody knows about bacteria, they are wise enough to realise some ingredients have real medicinal properties.

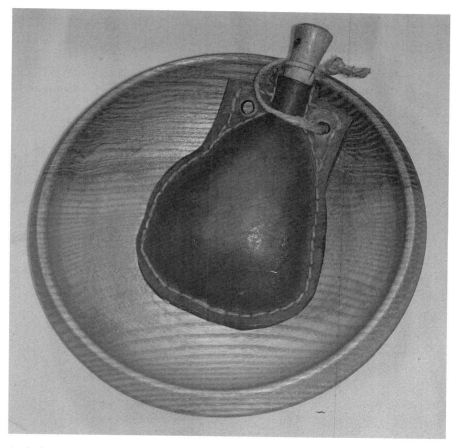

A vinaigrette bottle for your personal seasoning.

Top Tip

Ask for the 'bill' when you arrive. This is the 'bill of fayre' or menu, though there's probably not much choice. When you want the bill or check, ask for the 'reckoning'.

Preparation for your journey

I would advise, before you set out on your time-travelling adventure that you have a full medical and dental check-up and have your tetanus jab, your MMR jab and a few others, and take your anti-malaria pills, as if you were going to a third world destination. Medieval England is a third world country. Medical practice is more like witch-doctoring, sepsis is a daily risk and as for dental surgery, believe me; you want to avoid that at all costs.

You'll need to be fit. Just surviving the daily grind is hard enough, whether you're a lord or a labourer. And forget that diet you were thinking of going on. In a draughty stone castle in January, or a thatched hovel in March, you'll be burning 4,000-5,000 calories a day just working and keeping warm. So could you plan your journey for the summer months? The weather will be warmer, but there will be no air-conditioning, sun-protection factor 30 or drinks from the fridge, and fleas, bed bugs, lice and ticks will be around in their greatest numbers, as will the malaria-carrying mosquitoes.

You had better get used to the dirt. The concept of 'hygiene' means nothing: life is unsanitary; toilet facilities are minimal, communal and very smelly. The people aren't too fragrant either, though they do their best – as we shall see – but soon after your arrival you'll probably start to pong like everyone else and won't notice the stench so much. Sunday church services will probably be the most odoriferous assemblies you're likely to experience and attendance is compulsory, if you don't want to be fined or whipped around the churchyard in your underwear. Everyone goes to church, wearing their Sunday best, to honour God and outshine their neighbours' apparel if possible.

For the rest of the week, these much-valued clothes are hung where it's believed the moths will never find them: in the loo. Medieval folk think moths avoid the awful smell of a non-flushing toilet and that their clothes are safe there. The medieval word for an indoor convenience is 'garderobe' or, as we say, 'wardrobe', where robes are guarded or warded. No wonder they smell bad. Does that explain the Church's eager expenditure on incense as a means of perfuming the air around the congregation? The scented holy smoke is supposed to waft prayers heavenwards, but if it spares the priests' noses as well, so much the better. Mind you, the clergy smell no sweeter than anyone else, but fragrance is considered a saintly virtue. And after church, you'll get the best meal of the week.

If you are concerned about food-miles, put your mind at rest: in medieval England, food-miles for almost every daily staple are in single digits. Local produce is everything. There are no E-number additives and no chemical residues from herbicides, pesticides, fungicides or commercially produced fertilisers; there is only manure. But all is not perfect. Because all these things are lacking, fruit and vegetables suffer from blight, mould, mildew and every pest imaginable, and where human manure is used on the fields, intestinal parasites like tapeworms and roundworms can be passed on if vegetables aren't washed properly. Wheat, barley and oat yields are low because breeding programmes to improve cereal crops haven't been implemented. The sheep, pigs, goats, chickens and cows are small and scrawny for the same reason, although horses are an exception. Stud farms, usually run by monasteries, breed feisty destriers (warhorses), coursers (hunters) for speed, palfries for comfortable riding and workhorses, so the idea that animal types can be manipulated by man is catching on.

Do not expect tender lamb or plump chicken for Sunday dinner. Lambs grow into sheep with years of profitable wool production ahead of them. To slaughter a lamb is a waste of a valuable resource, but when the sheep is too old to breed and its fleece mangy, or if it dies of old age or accident, then it can be eaten. The resulting mutton will be tough and stringy and require boiling for hours. The same applies to chickens. Only after years of egg-laying is a hen put in the pot. Cows, too, are more important for milk production and bullocks (castrated bulls) for draught animals. In this case, pigs are the exception. No use for fleeces and, as far as I know, no one has ever milked a pig, so they are bred purely for food. Their meat can be roasted, smoked, pickled or salted and every household should have one. Brought as a piglet in spring, it is fed on scraps or left to forage for itself, then slaughtered in November to see a family through the winter, either eaten as preserved meat or the meat sold for money with which to buy other foodstuffs and necessities for the colder months. Suckling pig – a piglet that is so young it's still suckling from the sow – is a delicacy, usually spit-roasted, but unless you're consorting with lords, it's unlikely it will be on poor folks' menus.

For those of you who don't like to eat their greens, I advise you to make for a wealthy household where your preferences will be appreciated. The poor have cabbage (worts or caboshes or pot-herbs) with just about every meal, but the rich folk scorn such green stuff as peasant food. Better yet, at mealtimes, every course comes with both sweet and savoury dishes and if you choose to eat only the medieval equivalents of lemon meringue pie, cherry tart and sultana pudding with cream and custard, you will be regarded as a discerning diner indeed. No well-to-do mother tells her child to 'eat your greens'.

However, you will not find potatoes on the medieval menu: no mash, roasties or chips. I hope you like fish since this is compulsory at least twice a week and every day during Lent – the forty days leading up to Easter – unless you go vegetarian, or maybe vegan, in which case, no milk, cheese, eggs or butter are allowed either.

It is your duty to work

Medieval folk reckon it's your God-given duty to work, whether that work is supervising others, caring for their souls, labouring on the land or working at a craft. Only very small children, the severely disabled or bedridden can be excused from work of any kind. Unemployment receives little sympathy and beggars must be considered 'deserving' to be given any charity. So roll up your sleeves and prepare to earn your keep.

Early on in the Middle Ages there were thought to be only three 'estates' of man, each ordained by God and whichever you were born into, there you stayed. Otherwise, you were flouting God's will, to the peril of your soul. Either you were born into the fighting class, which meant you were wealthy but obliged to defend everyone else, or you

The three estates: 'Those who prayed; those who fought and those who laboured'.

were born a poor serf, working the fields to put food on the table for the wealthy, leaving just enough for yourself if the harvest was good. The third group was the clergy. In theory at least, no one could be born into this class because, from the year 1215, the clergy were forbidden to marry. Instead, the fighting class might have their younger sons become churchmen, as bishops and abbots. For the poor labourers, having a son become a priest, or a daughter a nun, was the only way to help them escape the lowliest class. In any case, it had to be God's will, like everything else in medieval life.

However, a new class is developing. They aren't professional fighters or priests, and agricultural labouring is not their main occupation.

These are the craftsmen and tradesmen, and towns grow up where such people come together to supply the local communities.

Potters, blacksmiths, spinners and weavers have always provided basic needs: cups, dishes and storage vessels; tools, weapons and horseshoes; textiles and clothing. But by the thirteenth century towns are home to more crafts than you can name, often specialists developed from these basic crafts. For example, the smiths or metalworkers have diversified. There are goldsmiths, silversmiths, coppersmiths, coin-strikers, arrowsmiths, bladesmiths, swordsmiths, cutlers, pewterers, armourers, makers of chainmail, lorimers who make decorations for horse-harness, farriers who shoe the animals and even plumbers who work with lead. The weavers have been joined by fullers and dyers, tailors and drapers, embroiderers and haberdashers, silk-women, glovers, tanners and whitawyers, skinners and furriers, cap-makers, purse-makers, shoemakers and fripperers who smarten up, repair and sell second-hand clothing. So, if you are artistic, perhaps one of these occupations could give you employment, although the guilds can make life difficult for any enterprising artisan, more on which later.

You may also join this great 'middling class' in a more professional capacity as a lawyer, a physician, or, if you have a good head for business, as a merchant. This latter profession is where money is to be made, if you're successful, but it's pretty much a case of 'men only need apply' for these jobs. Equality in the employment market doesn't exist, and in any job women get paid far less than men. Women need not despair, however. Although I have never come across a female lawyer in medieval records, there are a few women practising in various branches of medicine and a number successfully running businesses on their own account, as we will see. With your modern knowledge, you may be at an advantage in some professions, but one definite disadvantage is that imperial measures and pre-decimal coinage may be unfamiliar to you. I would advise you do a crash course on pounds, shillings and pence; ells, yards, feet and inches; stones, pounds and ounces, etc. before you go on your time-travelling adventure. Otherwise you could find life difficult and expensive.

If your handwriting is neat, you could get a job as a scribe, although you'll have to learn some odd letter shapes, strange capitals and some weird abbreviations. However, if your spelling isn't so good, don't worry:

consistent spelling is definitely optional. And this is one area where females can excel: in book production.

So now you have some idea of what sort of experiences to expect on your historical travels. If I haven't put you off too much and you still intend to go and visit your ancestors, we will now look in more detail at the pitfalls, things to be avoided and how to become one of the locals, blending in. There will be unusual laws to be obeyed and the language, Chaucer's Middle English, will sound very different – almost foreign to modern English ears – and words you recognise may not mean what you think they do. Hopefully, your questions will be answered as I reveal what you will need to know to survive in medieval England. I trust that you'll enjoy your visit.

Chapter 2

Social Structure and Housing

Class structure – how do the poor live?

In the introduction I mentioned that, in early medieval times, there were three social classes. They were described as 'those who fought, those who prayed and those who worked the land', the latter being by far the greatest in number. By the later medieval period there is an up-and-coming 'middling' class of tradesmen, craftsmen and merchants affecting the neat pattern of what was reckoned to be God's own perfect design. So where will you, a traveller in time, fit into the design?

Supposing you are destined to be the most humble of all: a serf. Not a peasant; England has never had peasants. *Paysans* is the French word meaning 'country-dwellers'. The English use the term 'peasant' to describe the poorest of their French enemies and mean it as an insult. Even the so-called 'Peasants' Revolt', which occurred in England in 1381, is a more recent name for the uprising. At the time, it is known as the 'Revolt of the Commons', i.e. common people. Even the term 'serf' is little used by the fourteenth century.

If you are a serf, you have my deepest sympathy. Your life will be hard, probably short and everyone will rank higher than you on the social ladder. Make sure you always wear a cap of some sort because you'll have to doff it, lower your eyes and bend the knee a little to everyone you meet, except those few who are worse off than you. You can always tell the status of men or women by their dress. Whereas you wear dull, colourless, shapeless garments of coarse homespun cloth, your betters – i.e. almost everyone else – will be clad in more colourful textiles. Dyes are expensive and so is quality cloth, so the robes of the wealthier classes are long, voluminous and brightly coloured. A word of warning though: King Henry II was known as 'curt-mantle' because he preferred to wear a short cloak so it didn't get in his way when he was rushing about. Therefore, length of garments is not an infallible indication of status. I'd advise taking your cap off to every man, just in case one of them happens to be a king.

Even this lowest social class has a hierarchy. A serf is not much better than a slave. He has his own hovel to live in but is 'unfree' and belongs to the lord of the manor. A serf works his lord's fields and tends the livestock. He can't marry or move away without his lord's permission. In exchange, his lord defends him in time of war and allows him to have enough of the foodstuff he grows to feed himself and his family.[1]

Above the serf is the villein or cottar. He has more freedom than a serf, although he still belongs to his lord, to whom he pays rent, and is tied to the manor. He lives in a better dwelling – a cottage – usually with a small plot of land attached where he grows vegetables and herbs, keeps chickens, a pig, and perhaps a goat for milk. He rents strips of land in the fields and payment is made by working the lord's strips and giving free labour whenever the lord demands it. This will be one or two days each week but with extra work demanded at harvest time – to the detriment of his own crops, which need harvesting too – help at lambing time or with sheep-shearing, ploughing and sowing seed. 'Rent' may also stipulate other duties, such as taking the lord's surplus crops to market, providing him with two chickens for his Christmas dinner, or a dozen eggs at Easter. However, sale of a villein's extra eggs, onions or cabbages, butter or cheese, or perhaps three days of ploughing not required by his rental agreement, could actually earn him a few coins; something a serf never has.

DID YOU KNOW?

When a villein died, his heir had to pay the lord a 'herriot', giving him his best animal, before he was allowed to inherit.

Only the most respected villein had the opportunity to be elected by his fellows as their reeve. This role was the forerunner of the office of mayor. Most villages had a reeve to represent the common folk at the lord's manorial court, where infringements of the law, property rights and tenancy agreements were dealt with. More serious offences, such as murder or kidnap, went to a higher court: the Shire-reeves', or Sheriffs',

Courts at county level and, ultimately, the King's Court. Crimes such as adultery, incest, swearing or non-attendance at mass on Sunday were heard by a Church Court.

This system was known as feudalism, introduced by the Normans, when William the Conqueror defeated the last Anglo-Saxon king of England, Harold Godwinson, in 1066. The system works well enough, repressive though it is, until the Great Pestilence arrives in 1348, resulting in too few serfs and villeins to do all the labouring and lords losing not only their workers but the rents they paid. Of the survivors, many leave their homes without the lord's permission, going in search of more favourable tenancies and the chance to earn higher wages. These villeins are, basically, breaking the law, and this is when the word 'villein' becomes 'villain', meaning a criminal. But there are so many of them in the later fourteenth century that the system can't punish them all and feudalism becomes a thing of the past. By the fifteenth century serfs are no more; villeins are known as tenants, mostly paying their rents in money and earning wages for their labour. The more affluent tenants buy up the bits and pieces of land abandoned by those who have died or left the village to seek work in towns. These tenant-farmers evolve into prosperous yeomen, well on the way to becoming gentlemen, further blurring the hierarchy as they marry into the higher classes.

The poorest live in one-room hovels, unless their lord is very generous. The walls are of wattle-and-daub, an ancient way of building. Wattle consists of woven panels of twigs, most often of willow or hazel, fixed to a wooden framework. The wattle is then covered with daub – a mixture of mud, animal dung and straw – smoothed on to fill any gaps. When dry, this mix will set hard like plaster and keep out the weather. It can be painted with limewash, which not only colours the daub white but helps prevent it growing mould, as well as putting off vermin to some extent, although it will most likely need annual repairs. Windows are simply gaps left in the wattle panels and are small and few in number to avoid losing warmth or letting in wind and rain. Wooden shutters cover these gaps at night and in the worst weather, so the hovel can be very dark. Window glass is reserved for churches and even the wealthy don't have glazed windows much before the fourteenth century.

The hovel is heated by an open fire in a central hearth on which the cooking is done. There is no chimney and the smoke escapes through the windows, doorway and gaps in the roof. The roof is probably thatched with reeds, if these grow locally, or with cut turves. At night and in cold weather any livestock you have will be brought inside to share your hovel. They may smell, but then so do you. In return for putting up with the stink and dung on the floor, you get the benefit of their extra warmth.

Bedding is very basic. A sack stuffed with straw – a paliasse – will be your mattress on the floor, with a blanket. If it grows locally, you can use bracken as the stuffing instead. Creatures like fleas and lice are not so keen to live in bracken. Hay, though softer, is not an option for your bedding since it is used to feed the animals in winter. Sheets and pillows are for rich folk.

Food, like all your amenities, is poor and plain. Your bread will be made of flour and water and is probably unrisen. The flour has to be ground from the grain grown in your lord's fields, which he lets you have a share of in exchange for your hard work. Wives and children are allowed to 'glean' the field after the cereals are harvested, collecting up any fallen ears of wheat, barley or rye, or tops off the oats for their own use. This tradition goes back to biblical times. This means your flour will often be a mixture of grains, along with the seeds of any weeds that also grew in the fields. These are mostly harmless but it's worth weeding the field well in summer, as your lord will require of you.

Top tip

Pay special attention to removing the pretty pink-purple flowers of corn-cockle, as its seeds are poisonous and will cause an upset stomach.

How you grind your grain to make the flour will be up to your lord. He may allow you to grind your own at home, using two quern-stones. This is hard work and usually done by women, kneeling on the floor. After years of doing this since childhood, women can develop an extra spur of bone on their heels which archaeologists may use to determine the sex of a partial skeleton just from a heel bone. You might think it's better to avoid grinding your own flour, and if your lord owns a mill he may well force you to use it. (Before around 1300 mills were water-powered; windmills were introduced from the Netherlands in the fourteenth century.) The Abbot of St Albans in Hertfordshire was so strict about this that he confiscated all his tenants' quern-stones and used them to pave his courtyard, so they had to go to the mill. Having ground your

Corn-cockle – make sure you weed this poisonous plant out of the cornfield.

flour for you, the miller takes a share of it in payment and so does the lord. When grain is scarce and vital for bread you can understand why poor folk prefer to grind their own. Incidentally, the tenants of the Abbot of St Albans have their revenge during the so-called Peasants' Revolt of 1381 when they dig up his courtyard and take back their grinding stones.

A mixture of flour and water can be baked into flatbreads on a hot hearth stone. Dried peas and possibly beans will also be part of your 'wages', like the grain. These are stewed up in a pot on the fire to make 'pottage', the thicker, the better. Pottage can be flavoured with any extra vegetables the lord allows you to take from his field, or plants that grow wild in the hedgerows. Wild carrots may be an option, but you need to know your plants well because wild carrot is very similar in appearance to hemlock water-dropwort and its cousins, which are deadly poisonous. Stinging nettles may not sound appetising but their fresh green tops taste like spinach and make a good addition to pottage.

Ale is the most nourishing and healthiest drink to go with your bread and pottage. Water can be polluted with animal droppings, or contain bugs invisible to the eye, or pathogens of one sort or another. Boiling water makes it safer to drink, and though nobody knows that at this time, brewing ale involves boiling the water and thus ale is, 'inexplicably', a safe drink. Even children drink the second and weaker brewing. The difficulty is that brewing malted barley into ale takes days to achieve and involves some expensive equipment such as vats and strainers. To overcome these problems, the equipment may belong to the village, rather than individual families, and passes to a different household each week so that they can each take a turn to brew ale for everyone. When a batch is ready for drinking, a bunch or twig of green leaves is put above the door and folk bring their jugs to be filled. Fresh ale is only drinkable for about a week before it goes sour, by which time another household has a fresh brewing ready to be shared around.

This is how village taverns begin. Travellers passing through the village also expect to be able to get a drink there, but will have to pay. In this way, a household may be able to buy its own brewing equipment and a store of barley, and gradually their house becomes a permanent tavern. But every brewing of ale, whether private or commercial, is subject to testing by the local ale-taster. This is a legal requirement and he – it's always a man, although women, known as 'brewsters', do the brewing – not only samples the ale to make certain the drink is palatable and not watered down, but checks the measuring cups to make sure customers aren't being swindled. The assize of ale is a countrywide set of regulations governing the drink.

The miracle of the honest brewster

There was once an ale-wife, a widow who made her living by brewing and selling ale. One day, her house caught on fire, threatening her livelihood and everything she possessed. Now, some might see this as an act of divine retribution, since it is well known that every ale-wife swindles her customers by serving them short measures and hence her kind are always being fined by the ale-tasters. But this particular ale-wife claimed to be honest and lined up all her measuring cups in the street outside her burning house so God could see them clearly and know they were true measures. Then she fell on her knees, beseeching the Lord to see her honest cups and save her house from the flames.

Seeing her plight, God sent a cloud to rain on her house and put out the fire, saving an honest woman's possessions. Was this a miracle? No. The true miracle wasn't God's timely intervention – for He can do this whenever He wishes – but rather the existence of a brewster who served her customers full measures.

Villeins or cottars have their cottages. Although these are often built of the same materials as the serfs' hovels, they usually have two rooms: one for the livestock and one for the people. The human half of the house may have a sort of mezzanine for use as a bedroom, reached by a ladder. Windows may be a bit larger and use oiled parchment to make semi-transparent coverings, or else thin sheets of horn. Either of these materials let in light and keep out the weather, but don't expect to admire the view from the window. Cooking facilities aren't much different from the serfs', but there may be more cups, bowls, dishes and spoons, all of treenware (wood) or cheap pottery. Perhaps some chicken feathers have been saved, 'baked' by the fire to remove parasites, and used to stuff pillows, while blankets can be of better quality.

The cottage will have a back door, out to the toft or garden. Here the villeins grow pot-herbs, such as onions and leeks, cabbages, parsnips, turnips, radishes and beets to extend their menu or to sell at market. Other herbs can include lavender to keep clothes fresh and deter moths, sage for flavouring and medicinal purposes, or meadowsweet to strew on the floor and perfume the air as well as being an excellent headache remedy. Furniture will be minimal: stools, benches and, if you're lucky, a bedframe.

Class structure – how do the wealthy live?

At whichever date you arrive, life will be more pleasant if you are rich; nothing has changed there. Under feudalism the lord of the manor is answerable and owes service in time of war to his overlord; perhaps a knight or a baron. He, in turn, is answerable in the same manner to an earl or a duke who, finally, answers to the king. Everyone, from the lowliest serf to the royal duke, ultimately owes their allegiance and service to the king. This doesn't always work out in practice, as happened at the time of King John (c.1215) during the Barons' War of the 1260s, the upheavals during Edward II's reign (1320s) and in the second half of the fifteenth century, at the time we call the 'Wars of the Roses', although this is a romantic name invented in the nineteenth century for a period of bloody, dynastic struggle.

The year is 1263. Let's ask Lady Eleanor, Countess of Leicester, about her life at Odiham Castle, Hampshire:

My lady, your husband, Simon de Montfort, Earl of Leicester, is currently at war with King Henry III who happens to be your brother. This must make things difficult for you. Tell us how you cope with living in this great castle.

We don't always live here. We move from castle to castle. My husband keeps me and our youngest children away from the scenes of conflict, for fear we be taken captive and used to force his surrender to the king. Simon believes sincerely that kings should answer to God for their misdeeds, like everyone else but, in this life, must rule righteously, as directed by the lords and shire knights. He even thinks townsfolk ought to have a say in government. But I digress.

Of course, we also move elsewhere when a castle requires cleaning, the latrines need emptying. Who wants to be here when that terrible task goes on? The stink! You can't imagine.

What about feeding your household?

We have the produce from our desmesne – the home farm – both stored and fresh, the villeins' rental payments in kind, as well as our own livestock for meat and the castle fishponds for fresh fish, plus our fishing rights on the river. Although the local abbey disputes our sole rights there.

But the local produce only supplies the basics. What about luxurious foodstuffs? So noble a household must surely be able to afford them?

Such impertinence! Of course we can afford them. Why, last Easter, I entertained two bishops and their retinues. The meals had to impress because Simon wanted me to persuade them to his cause. I sent to London, to the grocers and pepperers, to supply me with all manner of delicacies. I ordered six pounds weight of ginger from India, costing fifteen shillings. Eight pounds of peppercorns at eighteen shillings and eight pence and six of cinnamon costing six shillings. Did you know that cinnamon bark is washed downstream from the Garden of Eden itself? Or so the merchants say. I ordered just a pound of saffron, it being the most expensive spice, even though we grow it in England,

and that alone cost fourteen shillings. I debated whether to order cloves and nutmeg but the bishops don't deserve too much luxury. I settled for twelve pounds of sugar, six pounds of sugar mixed with mace, ten pounds of rice ... You look surprised.

I didn't know you ate rice, my lady.

Well, it is a luxury your sort can't afford but it's imported, like the sugar, from Cyprus – the island wrested for Christendom by Richard the Lionheart. But back to my order: I included twenty pounds of almonds at four shillings and tuppence and an Easter treat for Simon: a box of gingerbread but don't tell him it cost two shillings and four pence. He's a frugal man where his own pleasures are concerned and will berate my extravagance.[2]

Life is somewhat more comfortable for ladies like the Countess of Leicester. She has some degree of privacy, which the poor folk never have, with such luxuries as a bedchamber, a solar and a pleasure garden. The countess's brother, King Henry III, is the first English monarch to have private bathrooms built for himself and his queen at his favourite royal residences. Although beautifully tiled, the water still has to be heated and carried in by the bucketful by servants and emptied the same way, as there are no taps, plug-holes or mains drainage. Simon de Montfort disapproves of such decadence, so there are no bathrooms in his castles. He does like a bit of privacy in the bedchamber, though, and often joins his wife in hers, whenever he's not too busy fighting battles and organising government, and they produce a number of fine children. Tapestries adorn the walls, an improvement brought from Simon's native France. Wall paintings look beautiful enough but cannot keep out the draughts nor impress visitors so well as an expensive tapestry hanging.

The solar, rather like a private parlour, is the best room in the castle or manor house. As warfare becomes less of a concern in the fourteenth century, windows in the solar become larger, to let in more sunlight. This isn't wise, if you fear a trebuchet might lob a rock at your castle wall, but peace allows for more comfort. The solar may even have a glazed window as glass becomes a rich man's luxury, no longer used only to honour God in churches. Chimneys appear, the great hall and solar often being the first rooms to benefit from this innovation.

Solar of Stokesay Castle, Shropshire – a light and airy room for the lords & ladies.

Once there are chimneys, you don't have to rely on smoke finding escape through open doors, windows and gaps in roofs, so ceilings and upper floors become possible, as do well-fitting window casements, which can be opened or closed to suit the weather. Castles are becoming cosier, at least for the lord and lady, their family, friends and guests.

The solar is the room where the light is best and so ladies do their sewing and fine embroidery there. By the fourteenth century more and more people are literate, so the solar is a popular place for reading, either to yourself or, more likely as a shared activity, reading aloud to others.

DID YOU KNOW?

The famous writer, Geoffrey Chaucer, read his *Canterbury Tales* aloud to Richard II's court.

If the weather is fine, these activities can be taken outside into the pleasure garden. Quite different from a toft, where only useful plants are grown, the private, or privy, garden is meant to be enjoyed, with seats

23

and arbours for relaxing, or for having romantic assignations. Flowers are chosen for beauty, and perfume and water features – fountains or trickling brooks – provide a refreshing soundtrack. Songbirds are encouraged, or brought in cages if none come willingly, to serenade those relaxing in the shade of fruit trees, chosen for their springtime blossom, as well as autumn harvest. Bees are everywhere, pollinating flowers and making honey in their hives. Minstrels play and sing in this lovely haven, with dancing on the grass another happy activity, and children playing chase or hide-and-seek among the planting.

The great hall is the communal space of the castle or manor house. It may be large enough to accommodate hundreds in a large castle, or a couple of dozen people may be cramped in a lesser manor's hall. Originally, the hall was the only living room, used for eating, entertaining, holding court and sleeping but, as the medieval period progresses, the lord wants more privacy and separate rooms evolve for different purposes. Even as we reach the Tudor period, in 1485, the lord still dines in the hall when there are guests, rather than in his private apartments. Big occasions like Christmas will be celebrated in the hall, where everyone can eat together, enjoy the entertainments and dance. However, the lower servants – and this may include you – will be sleeping in the hall when the feasting and dancing is done. His lordship will likely still hold court here, too, perhaps four times a year, hearing pleas and petitions, adjudicating legal cases, approving marriages and new tenancies, etc.

Class structure – how do the middling sort live?

You may well find yourself among the 'middling sort', living in a town or even a city; London, Bristol, Norwich or York being the most important. Most town houses have their own garden plots where the women of the household grow vegetables and herbs for the pot, just like their country-dwelling sisters. Animals are often kept as well.

Compared to the labourer's hovel, your house in town may be quite comfortable, especially by the fifteenth century, as more people can afford to have chimneys and a few luxuries. Furniture is still sparse but appearing in a greater variety of forms in more homes by this time.

Do not tell a woman she looks nice; it's not a compliment. 'Nice' means too fussy and describes a wife who nags and finds fault. Don't say a child is naughty. 'Naughty' refers to being 'nothing; not even human' and describes murderers and rapists, not disobedient toddlers. However, even a clever child is 'silly' – it means sweet and innocent. Don't use the popular expression 'amazing' to describe a friend's efforts at cookery or carpentry or poetry. It doesn't mean marvellous but something as bewildering and confusing as being lost in 'a maze'. Astounding means that something hit you on the head so hard you see stars.

Having learned what words mean – and these are just a few that have changed – I advise you to keep quiet and listen when you first arrive at your historical destination. Ordinary folk are speaking English but it will sound like a foreign language, until you get used to it. Churchmen, doctors, lawyers and scholars may use Latin, and until the end of the fourteenth century, royalty and nobility speak a version of French. Into the fifteenth century French is far less fashionable, but it's still thought to be a sign of good breeding if you can speak it. One reason why you should say as little as possible to begin with is that your accent will mark you out as an alien, or foreigner.

Whether they are called strangers (from another village), foreigners (from another county with a different accent) or aliens (from another country with a different language) such people are always the most likely to be blamed for a crime or suspected of causing any local misfortune. If sheep go missing or the stream dries up, any visitor or newcomer is the first to come under suspicion. In a village, a stranger is immediately recognised because he isn't familiar and everyone knows their fellow villagers. Since such people don't look very different, unless their fashions are unique in some way, in towns incomers are generally identified by their accents.

In London in 1381, at the time of the Revolt of the Commons, along with those in authority, Flemings were a particular target for violence. These people from Flanders were invited here originally to set up weaving businesses as their special skills were valued. Gradually, however, because they stayed in the cities they were seen as denying employment to Englishmen. It was said that anyone who couldn't say 'bread and cheese' correctly must be a Fleming and was at the mercy of the mob. So be careful what you say and how you say it.

Chapter 3

Beliefs and Religious Ideas

In medieval England the Roman Catholic Church is involved in virtually every aspect of life. Religion is not just a matter of attending church services and saying prayers: it determines when you work, what you eat, how you dress and even when and how you may have sex! If you think the twenty-first century is ruled by Big Brother, with CCTV cameras everywhere, email and phone-tapping possibilities and DNA profiling, at least your bedroom remains private. The medieval church had no such reservations about imposing personal sanctions on everyday life.

One problem you'll face – along with most of the church congregation – is that the services conducted by the priests are all in Latin, so unless you've studied that language, it will be difficult to follow what's going on. Bibles, gospel books and mass books, as well as hymns and anthems sung by the choir, are also in Latin. In fact, it's a heretical act to have scriptural works in English. The reason given for this by the Catholic Church is that laymen cannot and must not attempt to understand God's words without a qualified priest to interpret and explain the meaning.

DID YOU KNOW?

Although he could read Latin, the Duke of Gloucester (b.1452, later Richard III, r.1483-85) owned a book of the Four Gospels in English, but required the permission of the Archbishop of Canterbury.

The priest conducts the Eucharist (also known as High Mass or the more modern Holy Communion) service every Sunday, but only he eats the wafer and drinks the wine, except at Easter when the congregation also receives wafers but still the wine is drunk by the priest alone.

Often, the congregation doesn't behave with much reverence, chatting, day-dreaming or even discussing business while the priest conducts the service. However, at the most sacred moment: the 'raising' or sanctifying of the Eucharist, a bell is rung to attract everyone's attention, the congregation stops talking, kneels and bows for a few minutes, after which the conversations resume. Being present is all that's required; it's not necessary to understand what goes on at the high altar but you'll get used to the routine: just copy what everyone else does. To end the service, each Sunday, a different household in the parish takes turns to provide ordinary bread to be blessed and shared by all.

If you fail to attend church at least once a week without a very good reason – wanting a lie-in on a Sunday does not qualify – you will be fined. Sickness, infirmity or a necessary absence from the parish are acceptable reasons for non-attendance. You will also be fined if you are found to have committed the sin of fornication (having sex before marriage), adultery (having sex with someone other than your spouse or with someone else's spouse) or – for women only – having an illegitimate child. If you are poor and 'belong' to the lord of the manor, getting married without his approval will result in a double fine, paid to the lord and the church. Punishments may not be financial but humiliating, instead. You will be 'shamed' in public.

Top tip

Before you travel back in time, learn the Lord's Prayer, the Hail Mary and, if you can, The Apostles' Creed by heart, in Latin. This knowledge will mark you as a good Catholic.

A popular parish event is the Church-ale. People either donate ale or the ingredients needed to brew a batch and then buy it back by the cupful. This is a way of raising funds for repairs to the church or perhaps to make a charitable donation to a local family that has fallen on hard times. The Church authorities aren't always as keen on these events as you might expect and sometimes attempt to ban them as being drunken and ungodly affairs. The parishioners often disagree and hold their Church-ale anyway, somewhere away from any holy building. The Church's funds mostly come from tithes. These are annual assessments of one tenth of the value of every household's 'moveable goods', payments to be made quarterly at St John's Day (24 June), Michaelmas (29 September), Christmas (25 December) and Lady Day (25 March). Moveable goods means anything that isn't part of the building, i.e. money, crops, livestock, furniture, clothes, jewellery, and in the case of merchants, anything stored in the shop or warehouse as well. The Church has so much power that at the Lateran Council meeting in 1215 Pope Innocent III was able to rule that tithe assessment and payment was to take priority over all other taxes and dues payable to emperors, kings, lords or anyone else.

Work and holidays

The Church also regulates your working life. In an era with few clocks and no personal time-pieces, how can you know when to get up, go to work, break for lunch, etc? The Church has the problem covered: bells.

DID YOU KNOW?

The connection between bells and time-keeping is so close the word 'clock' is a misspelling of the French word 'cloche', meaning 'a bell'.

Most towns and villages have at least one religious house – an abbey or friary or priory – close by, and the monks or nuns have bells rung to tell them when to go to the church to pray. Local people make use of the daytime bells as time-keepers, probably trying to sleep through the chiming of Matins and Lauds in the middle of the night. The bell for Prime, the first hour of the day, rings at 6am; Terce, the third hour, at around 9am; Sext at midday; Nones at 3pm; Vespers at around 6pm, but earlier in winter, and Compline rings at bedtime. There is also the Angelus bell that rings from your local church to tell parishioners when to get up, when to break for dinner and when to go to bed. The Angelus takes its name from the prayer you should recite on those three occasions, and begins: 'The angel said to Mary, "Blessed art Thou among women".' (In Latin the first word is 'Angelus').

Sunday being the Lord's Day and a day of rest, you must do no work except vital chores like feeding the animals, cooking meals and suchlike;

otherwise, the whole day should be given over to the contemplation of God and spiritual matters. This is considered so important the Church decrees that Saturday should be a half-day. Businesses and workshops close at midday so people can prepare for Sunday: making bread dough, chopping firewood, fetching water, peeling vegetables, getting their Sunday-best clothes ready for wearing to church the next day. The Church calendar includes numerous saints' days and feast days and many of these 'holy days' are holidays from work. Christmas, Easter, Whitsun and the moveable summer feast of Corpus Christi are among your days off, with other less religious events too, such as May Day and the Hocktide celebrations.

Hocktide is a tricky event to pin down, so you'll have to adapt to local customs, which differ from place to place. Hocktide begins on the Monday immediately following the second Sunday after Easter and is a day for men to have fun. The following day, Hock Tuesday, is when the women have the fun. On these days, the men and women alternately are allowed to take passers-by, usually of the opposite sex, as prisoners, demanding a kiss and a donation to charity as the cost of freedom. The churchwardens' accounts for St Mary-at-Hill, London, show that one year, on Hock Monday, the men gathered 14s 8d from the women and, on Tuesday, the women cajoled only 4s 5d from the men, perhaps collecting kisses, rather than coins.[1]

The Quarter Days, mentioned above as the dates when tithes must be paid, are also the days when rents and the king's taxes are due. Contracts for apprenticeships and other business agreements usually begin and end on a Quarter Day. Personal loans often fall due on those days too. The Royal Exchequer's financial year ends on Lady Day, 25 March, so all payments must be up to date by then, or penalties may be exacted.

DID YOU KNOW?

In 1752, when England's calendar had to miss out eleven days to bring us in line with the European calendar, the Exchequer refused to 'lose' eleven days' income, so our financial year had to end on 5 April instead and still does.

The Church calendar also relates to the three terms of the law courts and universities, beginning the legal and academic year at Michaelmas in late September (the autumn term), which ends at Christmas, then Hilary term (the spring term) beginning on 13 January (the feast of St Hilary) and ending at Easter, and Trinity term (the summer term). The feast of Holy Trinity is a moveable feast, dependent on the date of Easter, falling in late May to mid-June, Trinity Sunday being the first Sunday after Whitsun.

Fasting

The Church has different degrees of fasting or going without food. The most severe – a diet of bread and water – is given as a penance for sin. It's usually imposed for a day or two at the most, unless you're a candidate for sainthood, in which case you may choose to stick to this diet for the rest of your life. Your life is, therefore, likely to be short and such fasting isn't to be recommended.

The second degree of fasting is imposed by the Church on everyone, except babies and the sick, for the forty days of Lent leading up to Easter. The Lenten fast means eating no meat or animal products such as lard, no dairy, including milk, butter and cheese, and no eggs. Fish, bread and green stuff are on the menu but 'fish' includes some creatures you might not expect. Puffins, gulls and barnacle geese are thought to be born from the sea, so can be eaten as fish, along with seals, porpoises and whales, if any are washed up on a beach near you. Whales are supposed to belong to the king, officially, but he won't miss a flipper or two, and besides, the meat will have gone off by the time his highness gets to hear of the beast's demise.

The least stressful form of fasting simply means fish instead of meat on the menu with dairy produce allowed. I hope you like fish because the days requiring you eat it are numerous. Every Wednesday and Friday are fish days, the eve (or vigil) of every feast day and the whole of the Advent season, that is from the Sunday closest to St Andrew's day on 30 November until Christmas, including Christmas Eve. Since you're certain to need it, here is a fasting recipe for Lent that sounds quite tasty, although the poor won't be able to afford the pepper, sugar or almonds. Honey can replace sugar and hazelnuts, gathered from the hedgerow in autumn, and can also be saved and used in Lent instead of almonds. Weights and measures will be guesstimates and imperial, not precise.

Jowtes with Almond Milk

Take roughly 2 pounds weight of spinach leaves with stalks removed, 4 ounces of sliced green leaves of leeks and 2 large spoonfuls of chopped, fresh herbs, such as chives, thyme and hissop. Put all the green stuff in a cauldron with about 2 pints of water. Cook until the leeks are tender.

Meanwhile, take 4 ounces of ground almonds and a dash of flour in a small pot and add enough water to make a smooth cream. Drain the spinach mixture but keep the liquid. Chop any leaves that are too large to eat gracefully. Stir the almond cream into about half the cooking liquid and add salt, a dash of pepper, nutmeg and a pinch of sugar, if you can afford these luxuries. Return the cooked green stuff to the cauldron, simmer and stir until the mixture thickens. Now serve as a bright green soup.[2]

Almond milk, made as in the recipe above, but with boiling water or wine added instead of the soup juices, is a brilliant replacement for cows', sheep's or goats' milk. It can be used to thicken sauces or even make custard.

Sex

The Church would, if it could, ban sex altogether. However, since mankind would soon die out if it did, sex has to be regarded as a necessary sin. And it's very definitely 'a sin'. Monks and nuns must be celibate, though that isn't always the case. In 1434, when the Bishop of Lincoln visited Godstow Abbey, near Oxford, to check that nuns were being godly and keeping their vows, he had this to say: 'And that no nun [should] receive any secular [non-religious person] for any recreation in their rooms under threat of excommunication. For scholars of Oxford [university students] say that they can have whatever entertainment with the nuns they wish to desire'.[3] You can imagine what kind of entertainment they had in mind.

The Lateran Council of 1215, mentioned above, declared that priests must no longer have wives, nor even 'house-keepers'. It had always been the ideal that priests shouldn't marry, but many got around that by having live-in house-keepers who were wives in all but name. At that council the Pope made it official: no wives or 'house-keepers' allowed any longer. And while on the subject of clerical behaviour, the Pope decreed that for priests there must be no wantoness (sex with anyone of any kind), no drunkenness and they must not attend 'farces and histrionic exhibitions'; i.e. plays and theatrical performances. All these regulations are often ignored by many priests.

For married couples the sexual act is supposed to be banned on all fasting days, and because it is for the sole purpose of conceiving a child, it is not allowed if the women is already pregnant or breast-feeding, which is believed to prevent conception (although that's not guaranteed), or during her period.

DID YOU KNOW?

It's believed that a child conceived sinfully during menstruation will be marked for all to see because it will have red hair.

Even when sex is permitted only the missionary position, with the man on top, has Church approval and it must be done after dark, without candlelight, and eyes closed so you can't see your partner naked. And on no account must you enjoy yourself. It's a wonder we're not extinct.

If a child is conceived in accordance with Church doctrine, the woman still has a price to pay for her sin through the pain of childbirth, and if unmarried, she'll owe a *leyrwite* fine to the lord of the manor for bearing an illegitimate child. The child itself is born cursed by Original Sin until it's baptised. Unbaptised, the Church doesn't accept it as deserving Christian burial and it is condemned to spend eternity in Limbo, a region on the outskirts of Hell. For this reason, if a baby is likely to die before a priest arrives to baptise it, the midwife is allowed to perform this sacrament; the only holy office a woman may conduct. Sometimes, in the case of a still birth, it's not unknown for a midwife to swear the baby took a breath and baptise it, giving it a name, so it can be 'known' to God – officially, only the living can be christened – and spare it this horrible fate. Not surprisingly, because they can carry out baptisms, midwives are supposed to be scrutinised by the Church and granted a licence to practise, though not all bother. In an emergency, any woman may have to be a midwife.

What would be my beliefs about death and the dead?

Medieval people have a very different attitude to death than you may be used to in the twenty-first century. Death isn't a taboo subject to be mentioned in a whisper; it is an everyday fact of life, requiring discussion and preparation beforehand because you never know. By the

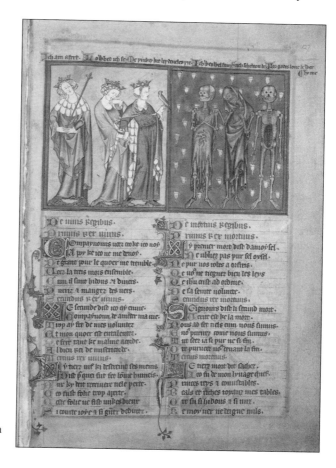

Memento mori –
The Three Living and
the Three Dead: 'As I am
so shall you be'.

fifteenth century, skeletons are a popular decorative theme on tombs and in wall paintings. The moral of the story is that however grand and important you are now, one day this will be you, so don't forget it. The occupant of the tomb is asking the viewer to pray for his soul now, in the hope that when the viewer's time comes, others will do the same for him. Known as *memento mori,* the skeletons are 'reminders of death': the destiny that awaits us all.

An English poet of the time, John Lydgate, wrote a piece on the subject, *The Dance of Death*. Here is an extract:

> O you people, hard-hearted as stone
> Who to the world devote all your attention
> As if it should last forever and anon.
> Where is your reason? Where is your wisdom?
> To see afore you the sudden violence
> Of cruel Death, who is so wise and sage,
> Who slays all by stroke of pestilence
> Both young and old, of low and high decent.
> Death spares not low or high degree
> Popes, Kings nor worthy Emperors.

The poem rhymes when read in its original Middle English. It is a comic-tragedy as Death invites everyone to join his dance, and whether nobleman or labourer, they all try to avoid the inevitable for as long as possible. But no amount of wealth or hard work can buy a way out. Death dances with them all in the end.

In medieval England, as I've said before – but it's such an important fact, it's worth repeating – daily life revolves around the Roman Catholic faith. This means there may be some unfamiliar concepts you'll need to get your head around, especially those which concern what happens after death. For good Christians, the body is buried in consecrated ground and there it stays, gradually returning to dust, though that isn't the end of the story, as we'll see shortly. More important to the medieval mind is the question of what happens to the soul. Whatever your personal beliefs in the twenty-first century, you'll have to accept that in this era of history, everyone has a soul.

After death, unless you're already destined for sainthood, in which case your soul will go straight to Heaven, or guilty of a heinous crime that can never be forgiven, in which case it'll go straight to Hell, your soul will go to a place called Purgatory. No one knows quite where it is but it's a sort of waiting room between Heaven and Hell. Here the souls of those who died in a godly condition can be further purified by suffering temporary punishment, having their sins utterly purged away – hence Purgatory – in preparation for entering Heaven. The time a soul must spend there can be reduced by the actions of the living. The Church has numerous possible ways of achieving this, most of which also help fill Church coffers.

Last wills may bequeath money to pay priests to pray for the soul of the departed and his family and friends and 'all Christian souls' are often included. Paying for masses to be said, fasting or even going on a pilgrimage in the name of the departed could all help the soul in Purgatory. Giving alms to the poor while you lived, or in your will, or paying for roads and bridges to be repaired are other social benefits that reflect upon the soul. Indulgences are another Church money-spinner. Supposedly issued by the Pope, you can buy these little pieces of paper for whatever you can afford and they promise your soul a sort of 'time off in lieu' in Purgatory, if you recite so many Paternosters (the Lord's Prayer) and so many Ave Marias (Hail Marys) now. But beware: these are often forgeries.

Whatever happens to the soul in Purgatory, eventually Judgement Day will come for all mankind. At the sound of the last trumpet, the bodies of the dead will be whole again and rise up from the grave to be reunited with their souls. But not all will qualify. Those unbaptised babies in Limbo, suicides, witches, heretics, hardened criminals and traitors who had their heads removed will not rise again. Everyone else will stand before Christ to be judged suitable for Heaven or be condemned forever to hellfire. This is serious stuff and you had better believe it because everyone else does.

DID YOU KNOW?

There was much serious scholarly debate about what would happen on Judgement Day to Christians who had drowned and been eaten by crabs and fish, which, in turn, were caught and eaten by other Christians as this meant that parts of the dead now formed part of others' bodies.

How would I deal with death?

Death is always distressing for loved ones left behind, and unexpected death is a daily possibility. There is even a special saint to guard you against an untimely demise. Most churches have a statue or wall painting of St Christopher facing the main entrance, so first thing each morning, parishioners can pop their heads around the door to greet the saint and say a quick prayer, asking for his protection from sudden death that day.

Hopefully, for those whom the worst befalls, a priest will be summoned in time to hear their final confession and grant absolution for their sins. Whether or not this happens before the dying ceases to breathe, a priest will administer the last rites, anointing the body with holy oil to ensure the good Christian soul has the best chance of getting into Heaven on Judgement Day. The body is then washed by the womenfolk, sprinkled with holy water by the priest and wrapped in a shroud. Until around 1300, coffins are rare and so the shrouded body is laid on a draped bier and carried to the graveyard for burial.

A medieval wall painting of St Christopher.

Funerals always take place after dark with a procession by torchlight – men only attending – from the house of the deceased to the church. It is traditional for the priest to dig the first spadeful of earth for the grave, after which the sexton and his lad take over the hard work. After 1300, the better off folk have coffins made to measure for the funeral and burial. The poor have to make do with the recycled parish coffin, the shrouded corpse being removed for burial and the box reused for the next pauper's funeral.

Since there are no facilities for cold storage of bodies, funerals take place as soon as possible, within in a day or two of death, unless the ground is frozen hard or snow-covered. With communications being slow – no instant messaging or phone calls – there is rarely time enough for distant friends and family to come to the funeral. This problem is overcome by the medieval 'month-mind', a sort of memorial service and feast held four weeks after the death, so that relatives can prepare and make the journey.

A stylish send-off

The Cely family were London wool merchants. When old Richard Cely died in 1482, the family commemorated him in a series of feasts, making sure their position in London society was properly recognised. For the month-mind feast, a cook and two spit-boys were hired at a cost of 12d, but in order that the guests should be suitably impressed, the Celys also hired Thomas Lyn, a professional butler, for 16d. At the year's mind feast, twelve months later, which ended the period of mourning, a cook named Wylchyr, or Wylshyre, was paid the considerable sum of 13s 4d for his services, but he must have been worth it because the family hired him again the following year, when Richard's widow, Agnes, died. A family friend, William Maryon, was paid to take care of the arrangements for this funeral feast. Having calculated the quantities needed, he ordered wild fowl from Collett the poulterer, various meats from Croke the butcher and spices from William Dygon the grocer. To impress the guests, the Celys also hired sixteen sets of pewter dishes for the occasion.

The 'year-mind' feast marks the anniversary of the death. Traditionally, the bereaved spouse can now set aside mourning and, if appropriate, consider remarriage, though not all wait quite that long. Widows with young children may need the support of a husband as soon as possible; wealthy widows may be snapped up by an eager new husband. One woman who has experienced this situation is Joanna Gedney:

> Widow Gedney, greetings. You've had experience of widowhood and remarriage. Can you tell us something of your life?

I've outlived four husbands, all good men. I'll remember each of them in my will, leaving 100 marks for priests to say masses for their souls. My first was John Gade and by him I had a daughter, Denise. My second husband, a widower, Richard Turnaunt, was a step up the social ladder. We lived in Winchester and he was a successful fuller in the cloth business. He became mayor of that city twice and an MP five times. I was a proud wife and when we had a son in 1428, I insisted he was called Richard, after his father. Sadly, I was widowed again in 1433, but Richard was much older than me. He left me quite wealthy and I wanted a new start for me and my son, Dick. There were too many memories in Winchester. Poor little Denise had died of the measles the year before.

What did you do then?

I came to London and wed Robert Large. The name suited him: large as life he was, and a rich mercer. I knew Robert slightly because Richard had dealings with him through the cloth trade. We liked each other, so marriage seemed sensible. Robert became Lord Mayor of London in 1439, so I was his Lady. When he died two years later, he left me his business and four apprentices – including William Caxton, of whom I expect much in the future – along with 4,000 marks! Can you believe such a sum? With that, I decided I didn't need another husband so, to ensure nobody pestered me to marry, I took a vow of perpetual chastity before the Bishop of London. But then a friend of ours, a prosperous draper and alderman, John Gedney, with whom I was co-executor of Robert's will, thought to improve both our estates. We each owned considerable properties in the village of Tottenham in Middlesex County; John suggested we combine our assets there and marriage was the simplest way. I reminded him of my vow but he said it didn't matter. We wed in 1442 but the scandal was terrible. We had to do penance and pay fines in the Church Court.

But you lived down the shame of it?

Of course. John became Lord Mayor of London – twice – after our marriage, so I was a mayor's lady again.

I think I loved John best of all. Since his death in 1449, I'm definitely not marrying again and intend to be buried beside him, when my time comes. Until then, I'm the Lady of the Manor of Tottenham with a fine house 'Le Ledenporche' in Threadneedle Street in London. When I'm gone, I'll leave a goodly sum to my son, Dick, but most of my wealth will go to his daughter, Thomasina. She'll be the next Lady of Tottenham and have all my lovely jewellery too. I hope she enjoys her inheritance for many years.[4]

One reason Joanna has done so well is that, according to London custom, upon a husband's death, after his funeral expenses are paid and his debts settled, the remainder of his property is divided into thirds: one third to church and to charity; one third to his widow; and one third to be shared among the children. Sometimes, a will may specify bequests otherwise, but if it seems unfair, this could be contested in the Church Courts.

How would I worship?

Pope Innocent III, at that famous Lateran Council of 1215, stipulated a change in how you should pray. Before that, everyone prayed standing up with their arms spread wide, ready to receive and embrace God's blessings. But as we saw in the introduction, at that time Europe's population was approaching its maximum. Churches were becoming crowded and praying in this way meant your neighbours were in danger of getting a poke in the eye or whacked across the ear. The Pope decided that it would be safer, take up less space and look tidier if the congregation prayed on their knees, with the palms of their hands pressed together. And so it was from then on, although priests and those conducting the services continued to pray with open arms, as some still do in the twenty-first century.

This council also recognised a new attitude towards communicating with God. It used to be thought that ordinary people's prayers, spoken in English or French, or whatever their natural language happened to be, never reached God's ears. He only listened to Latin, despite being all-knowing, strangely. Therefore, your prayers had to be translated into

Latin by a priest, who would then pass them on to God. However, this idea was being challenged. Ordinary people were daring to speak to God for themselves, believing He would hear and understand their prayers in any language. The Church had to accept that personal prayer was becoming popular, especially among women who might want to talk to the Almighty about matters unfit for a priest to hear. But women, being disorganised creatures, so it was thought, needed help to say their prayers in the correct order. St Dominic had recently invented rosary beads to aid the women and children in keeping count of their prayers to God and the Virgin Mary and the council gave the rosary papal approval.

Chapter 4

Clothing and Appearance

In medieval society nothing indicates your status as much as what you wear, so you'll need to get this right. T-shirt, jeans and trainers will have to be left behind in the twenty-first century, I'm afraid, and if you are female, so will trousers, pants, culottes or shorts of any kind. For you, skirts are now compulsory. And so are hats or head-coverings of some sort for men and women, even in bed, and if you are a tradesman or a housewife you'll need to wear an apron too. Women often have a Sunday best apron, traditionally dyed blue with a plant called woad, to wear to church. Your apron is your badge of respectability, so wear it always and with pride. In 1463-64, Edward IV passed a law forbidding prostitutes from wearing aprons so they couldn't pretend to be respectable wives.

DID YOU KNOW?

'An apron' was originally 'a napron', a table napkin worn so you didn't spill soup down your front. This transferred 'n' also happened to 'noak' trees and 'noranges'.

Sumptuary Laws

Put simply, Sumptuary Laws are legal acts, first introduced in the fourteenth century, with the sole purpose of averting the chaos caused by people of lower rank dressing above their status. This may sound like nonsense to us in an age when you can go ahead and wear a designer label if you can afford it. We also take for granted the barging and the elbows in the ribs; characteristics of rush hour commuting. But back in medieval times, when few commuted farther than a couple of streets away to their place of work, what we accept as normal rush hour behaviour would probably have resulted in the militia being called out to quell the riot.

In medieval England it just isn't done to put your head down and plough your way along, regardless of your fellows on the street. There are rules of etiquette to be observed by everyone. And that's why sumptuary laws are needed.

The way people conduct themselves when out and about is determined by their status. Everybody makes way for the king. If you are on horseback, you must take your beast aside, off the road, to allow the king to pass unhindered, removing your headwear and bowing. If on foot, you also get out of the way, take off your cap and bend the knee to your sovereign. In fact, you are required to make way for everyone who is your social superior and those below your status will step aside for you and doff their hats. But how can you tell who is where on the social ladder in relation to you? If every Tom, Dick and Prince Hal wears silks, velvets and ermine, dyed deep blue (what we would call 'royal blue'), crimson or imperial purple, the entire system collapses. That is why it matters so much what you wear, how you dress and the reason sumptuary laws exist.[1]

In the fourteenth century the first raft of sumptuary legislation was passed at the request of various nobles who – to their great disgust – saw merchants on the streets of London who were more richly dressed than they were. Humble folk, in confusion, were stepping aside for these merchants and doing them greater courtesy than the less finely clothed lords. This was insupportable. Breeding outweighed wealth, the lords complained, and it wasn't their fault that the more successful merchants could afford a better wardrobe than theirs. The later fourteenth century being hard times for nobles, what with their rent-paying tenants and waged labourers dying of plague and the survivors demanding lower rents and better pay, the lords were not so impressively attired as before.

When King Richard II married Anne of Bohemia in 1382 she brought an entourage with her from her homeland along with new fashions and ideas. Anne is thought to have introduced the side-saddle as a more elegant way for ladies to ride. Her Bohemian gentlemen wore shoes with long, pointed or 'piked' toes. The English also called them 'cracows' because they had been invented in Krakow, then in Bohemia

with envy. After church, Alice goes to the sheriff and reports that her fellow parishioner is dressing far above her status. That afternoon, the sheriff visits Jane, demands that she hands the offending gown over to him and her husband must pay a fine of sixpence. The money goes into the city coffers but what about the gown? That is given to Alice as her reward for having reported Jane, even though Alice's husband is only a cutler and, therefore, she is no more entitled to wear it than Jane. Yet the following Sunday, Alice wears the gown of crimson camlet to church. Jane reports her to the sheriff; the sheriff gets another sixpence in the coffers and Jane gets her gown back to wear next week. And so on ...

Anyone who isn't a lord's son, a government servant or a gentleman with an income from land of at least £100 per annum is forbidden to wear velvet, satin or damask. If their land is worth £20 or more then satin, damask or camlet can be used to line or trim their clothing, but not for the main body of the garment. The problem is that into the fifteenth century more and more successful merchants are becoming richer than the aristocracy. Inter-marriage makes matters even more complex. The nobility want to share in the mercantile wealth, and merchants yearn for titles and high status. The solution is for a lord's penniless second and untitled son to wed the daughter of a rich merchant, but where do their offspring stand on the social ladder? The children aren't the sons and daughters of a lord and yet they can now afford to live in more opulence than their paternal relatives who still have titles. An additional oddity concerns the way in which wealth is judged. Annual income from land is always regarded as having greater status than the same monetary income gained from trade. The sumptuary laws passed in the reign of King Edward III, in 1363, equate a landowner worth £200 a year to a merchant worth £1,000. No wonder the laws are flouted.

Attempts to mark out prostitutes from respectable women, included in Edward III's and Edward IV's sumptuary laws of 1363 and 1462-63, insist that women in the sex trade should wear unlined striped hoods (and no aprons). It is also the custom that a married woman must cover her hair: a 'loose' woman, i.e. one wearing her hair loose and uncovered, is of easy virtue and up to no good. The frequency of acts and the huge number of laws passed proves that the authorities are losing the fight to preserve social distinctions, as well as attempting to maintain morals and ethics, preserving the English economy against foreign imports, or restraining the excesses of fashion. However, a good many of the various sumptuary laws dating back to as early as the fourteenth century were still on the English statute books as recently as the 1800s, and some may even remain. Am I a loose woman because I didn't wear a head-covering to the supermarket this morning, for example? Or were we allowed to eat meat dishes on five days last week? The sumptuary laws covered what you could eat, as well as what you could wear, and those of lower status were not allowed to have meat very often.

What kind of clothes would I wear?

Your clothes would be made of natural fibres, such as wool and linen, silk, if you're of high status, or textiles that are a mixture of these. No 'easy-care', 'non-iron', 'permanent-press' or 'drip-dry', I'm afraid, although everything is non-iron because irons haven't been invented yet. Any woollen clothes are hardly ever washed in any case, though this isn't such a bad thing, as we'll see. Linen garments, sheets, tablecloths and napkins and such like are pulled straight while wet from laundering, dried and then folded neatly and put into a press, and left until needed. If done properly, the items will come out smooth, wrinkle-free and 'pressed'. From my own experience as a historical re-enactor, I can confirm that natural fibres are wonderful to wear, if you do so correctly. They are comfortable, warm in winter and cool in summer.

Because woollens are difficult to wash, becoming sodden and heavy if immersed, and, therefore, get pulled out of shape and may shrink, it's important to prevent them becoming soiled to begin with. For this reason it is virtually unknown to wear wool next to the skin where it would become sweaty and smelly. Linen underwear is a must and most people change it every day, except for the poorest folk who can't afford spare clothes. Rich people with extensive wardrobes may change their undies two or three times a day: because they can afford to and don't have to do their own laundry. For women, and children of both sexes until they are toilet trained, underwear consists of a kind of long linen smock, sometimes called a shift or a chemise. Lengths may vary but around knee-length for children and mid-calf or longer for women, usually with long sleeves. The shift protects the skin from chafing by any woollen outer garments and freely absorbs sweat, protecting the clothes worn on top.

An experiment carried out by Ruth Goodman during work on a recent TV production entailed her living, dressing and working as a Tudor farmer's wife for three months. Clothes were much the same as pre-sixteenth-century ones. Ruth washed her hands and face frequently, but bathing, showering, perfumed toilet soap and deodorants weren't allowed. She changed her linen undergarment and headwear once a week, her woollen hose once a month, yet remained perfectly acceptable to the twenty-first-century film crew. Unlike one of her fellow re-enactors who showered daily, and used shampoo and deodorant but wore the same Tudor-style underwear throughout filming. Apparently he became more and more unpopular as the production went on as he smelled bad despite his personal hygiene procedure. Ruth smelled of wood smoke from the open fire but was otherwise quite socially acceptable.[3] So don't forget: change your underwear as often as you can.

It used to be thought that, for medieval women, there were no such things as bras and knickers, despite a couple of medieval manuscripts referring to 'breast-bags', possibly as being worn, well-padded, by prostitutes to enhance their assets. But in Lengberg Castle in Austria, in 2008, discoveries were made that required new thinking. Beneath the floorboards, put in place in the fifteenth century, the space had been packed with rags to reduce draughts and noise. Amongst the rags were found bras and tie-at-the-hips briefs.[4]

Medieval men wear undershirts and something like baggy boxers, held up with a draw-string, all of linen. Remember, there is no elastic, so everything has tapes, ties, pins or lacings. Over the undershirt a man may choose to wear a second shirt, perhaps with embroidery or trimmings that are meant to show. This won't be worn next to the skin, otherwise it will need frequent washing, which will spoil the decorative features.

In medieval England everyone wears hose or stockings. For men, these are long enough to be able to tie them to the bottom hem of the undershirt. Split-hose can be virtually a pair of trousers (pants) in two halves, tied to the shirt at the sides and with a cod-piece to cover any embarrassment. This is just a modest flap, tied in place, until Henry VIII turned the cod-piece into a 'huge' fashion statement in the sixteenth century. If he hadn't been king, he would probably have been a laughing stock.

Women's hose tend to be shorter, just over the knee and held up by garters, which are either tied in place or, for the better off, come with buckle-fastenings.

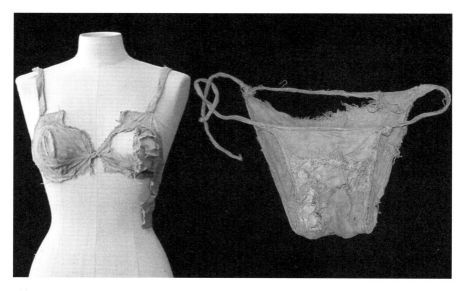

Fifteenth-century bra and briefs found at Lengberg Castle, Austria.

Order of the Garter

The Most Noble Order of the Garter, the most prestigious order of chivalry, was founded by King Edward III in 1348. He had in mind an idea of refounding King Arthur's Round Table. The emblem worn by the twenty-four knights of the order is a lady's garter. The story goes that the king was dancing with a lady when her garter slipped down to the floor. Courtiers sniggered, thinking the king must have been playing with her garter but he picked it up and fastened it around his own leg, saying '*Honi soit qui mal y pense*' ('Shame on him who thinks evil of this'). This phrase became the order's motto, but who was the embarrassed lady? No one knows for certain.

What you wear on top of your underclothes will depend on the fashions of the day and your wealth. In winter, they may well be made of wool or wool mixed with other fibres such as silk, if you're rich. In summer, linen and silk are cooler to wear. For women, a long tunic or kirtle is usual, with an over-gown or surcoat on top. Fashions change:

gowns are girdled (belted) at hip-level for much of the medieval period but high-waisted styles are in vogue in the fifteenth century. Sleeves may be tightly fitted or long and flowing and are sometimes removable, simply being tied to the gown at the shoulder. A most acceptable gift from your lover is a pair of detachable sleeves that can be worn with any of your gowns.

For men, a short top such as a rough jerkin is worn by common folk, or, for the fashionable beau, a stylish doublet goes over your shirt. Above that, you may wear an over gown. Lengths vary greatly, according to your age and what's in fashion. Generally, young men wear short gowns – sometimes indecently so – while older men like to keep their knees warm in longer gowns. Floor-length robes are also a way to show your wealth because far more cloth is used.

If money is no object, your outer gown, which everyone will see, should be of the most expensive textiles: exotic imports such as silk, velvet, satin, taffeta, brocade, damask and, of course, cloth-of-gold. This last comes in a variety of colours, with gold thread being woven through silk on the loom. The most expensive dyes are crimson, a vivid blue (like royal blue though that doesn't exist yet) and purple. Towards the end of the fifteenth century black becomes a big fashion statement. Not only is black dye very costly, it fades quickly so anyone wearing a truly black gown must be clad in a new ensemble and have servants to keep it free of dust flecks, lint and dandruff.

For cold weather, furs are essential as linings and trimmings. The sumptuary laws tell you which ones you may wear. Cat fur is so humble that anyone can wear it, but many furs are imported from the Baltic lands. Black sable, white fox, ermine (from a stoat in winter coat) and miniver are some of the most prestigious furs. Miniver, or 'ver', is the white belly fur of a red squirrel.

DID YOU KNOW?

In the French fairytale 'Cinderella', the heroine wore glass slippers to the ball. In fact, they were 'ver' slippers; an English misprint translating them as 'verre', which is French for glass. How could you dance in glass shoes?

Lacings

For women, how you fasten your gown tells everyone a great deal about you. Gowns could be laced down the front, down the back or at the sides. In an age when the Church teaches that it's God's will that families should have as many children as possible and contraception is not only wicked but unreliable anyway, married women are frequently pregnant. Side lacing is ideal maternity wear, adjusting it more loosely to suit an expanding waistline. Back lacing takes a bit of ingenuity, threading the laces through the eyelets before wriggling into the gown, but it is possible to do it yourself. More often, back lacing is a sign of a lady with maids to assist her in dressing. Front lacing is the most popular means of fastening, and buttons tend to be for decoration.

Just as with lacing up shoes, there are two ways of front lacing. The quickest way is to begin with two ends of equal length in the bottom two eyelets, then work your way up, crossing the laces between threading them through each pair of eyelets. To get the gown on and off, the laces can simply be loosened without unthreading. The second method is slower. With one short end passed through a top eyelet, the long end goes to the bottom and is spiral laced through each pair of eyelets to the top where it is tied to the opposite short end. This produces horizontal lines of lacing, not crosses. Respectable women use this more time-consuming method, and are 'straight-laced', as opposed to prostitutes, who use cross-lacing because they need to dress and undress often and quickly.

Where would I get my clothes?

When you first arrive in medieval England, hopefully you will have thought to wear something appropriate so that you can look the part. However, if you find your clothes are way out of fashion, I suggest you find a fripperer. Fripperers sell second-hand clothing, but don't worry, there is no shame in wearing other people's cast-offs. Clothes are often bequeathed in wills, handed down to children and servants, given to the Church, or otherwise worn until they are rags. A good fripperer will have given the clothes a proper brushing, sponged out any stains and carried out minor repairs, if necessary. Choosing from what he or she has on offer is the only way to buy 'off the peg' if you're in a hurry for a new outfit.

In the early fourteenth century clothes are at their most expensive because England doesn't yet produce her own textiles. Famous English wool is all exported, much of it to Flanders and the Netherlands, where it is processed and woven into cloth and imported back to England. For this reason even royalty had to economise. In her exchequer accounts, Queen Isabella, wife to Edward II, shows that when the hems of her long gowns became frayed from dragging along the floor, she had new hems put onto the old gowns. In fact, replaceable hems could just be pinned in place. Later in the century, Queen Philippa of Hainault, wife to Edward III, persuaded some of her countrymen to bring their weaving skills to England from Flanders and teach the English how to make their own woollen cloth. After that, clothes began to get cheaper; woollen ones, at least.

Buying new clothes is a slow business. First, you must visit a mercer. Mercers deal in cloth, from home-grown woollen textiles of various qualities to those exotic imports mentioned earlier. Having chosen the material, bearing in mind the sumptuary laws and with some idea of the garment you want, the mercer will advise you how much cloth you need. Be aware that he will likely suggest you buy rather more than required to boost his sales, so you may wish to set a limit on price before you start.

Once you have your cloth you take it to a tailor. He will know what necklines, waistlines and sleeve designs are being worn at the king's court and can produce more practical, day-to-day versions for ordinary folk. He may have small replicas ready-made to show you. Whatever style you decide on, the tailor will need to measure you for height, width of chest and waist, arm-length and, for men particularly, leg-length. There are no tape measures. Each customer has their own measure, a length of cord with their name on it and knotted to mark the size of each measurement. With this information, the tailor is ready to mark out your cloth, cut it and stitch it. Keeping any off-cuts of unused cloth is often a perk of the tailor's craft, so if you hope to make a matching purse from what is left, you need to make sure this in included in the deal, though it

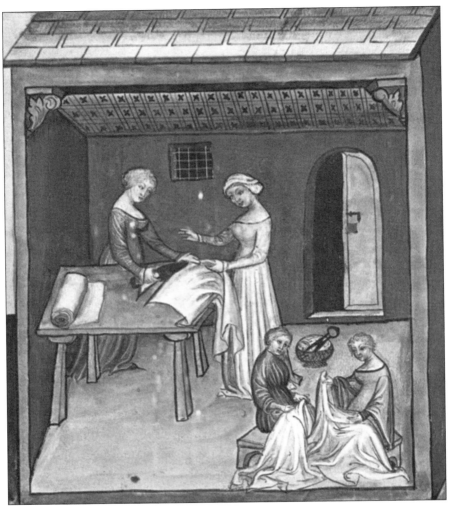

A tailoress cutting cloth and stitching garments for a customer.

will increase the price. Or the price could be reduced a little if you allow the tailor to use other off-cuts for cuffs or trimmings. Once the garment is tacked together you may need to go for a fitting before it's finally sewn together, all by hand, of course.

If you want woven braids, ribbons or other decoration you must supply them to the tailor. Such things can be purchased from a haberdasher or a silk-woman could make them to order for you. You can understand why new clothes take time.

How would I look after my clothes?

Having waited so patiently and gone to such trouble to have a new gown, it will be worthwhile taking great care of it. As we saw in the introduction, it is thought that hanging your fine clothes in the garderobe keeps the moths away. Wearing a good-sized apron to protect it is wise if you're a housewife or a craftsman.

Top tip

The Goodman of Paris, c.1395, advised his wife to treat grease marks and stains on his clothes with white wine or white vinegar.

John Russell, in his fifteenth-century *Boke of Nurture,* written between 1460 and 1470, has these instructions for keeping your clothes in good shape: '*In the warderobe ye must muche entende besily the robes to kepe well and also to brusche them clenly with the ende of a soft brusche ... and yet ouer moche bruschynge werethe cloth lyghtly. Lett neuer wollyn cloth ne furre passe a seuennyght* [a week] *to be unbrosshen and shakyn, tend therto aright, for moughtes* [moths] *be redy euer in them to gender* [breed] *and alight; therfore to drapery* [cloth] *and skynnery* [furs and leathers] *euer haue ye a sight.*'

As you'll realise, keeping your clothes in good order takes some effort, but they will last a long time; long enough that they are often bequeathed in people's wills.

How would I look after my skin and hair?

Although in the twenty-first-century it seems to be thought that medieval people were dirty and never bothered to wash, you will find this isn't the case. Every morning you will be expected to wash your face, hands and neck, at the very least, and often your feet as well. Mealtimes require elaborate hand-washing before, during – if necessary, making use of finger bowls – and at the end of the meal.

Top tip

If you cannot bear to be without a deodorant, the apothecary sells pieces of alum stone, which, if wetted, can be applied underarm and left to dry.

Bathing happens less frequently, mainly because of all the trouble required to heat so much water, bucketful by bucketful, and the same to empty the tub afterwards. But, of course, if you're royal you have servants to do that for you. King Henry III even had a purpose-built tiled bathroom installed at his palace at Clarendon in Wiltshire. King John bathed once a fortnight – even in winter – paying his bath-man 13d on bath-night, instead of the usual 5d per day, because of the extra work involved.

For lesser folk, a half barrel lined with linen sheets to avoid splinters, and a stool to sit on, served the purpose. Here are John Russell's instructions for preparing and giving your husband, lord or anyone else a bath:

> If your lord wishes to bathe and wash his body clean, hang sheets round the roof, every one full of flowers and sweet green herbs, and have five or six sponges to sit upon, and a sheet over so that he may bathe there for a while, and have a sponge also for under his feet, if there be any to spare, and always be careful that the door is shut. Have a basin full of hot fresh herbs and wash his body with a soft sponge, rinse him with fair rose water, and throw it over him; then let him go to bed; but see that the bed be sweet and nice; and first put on his socks and slippers that he may go near the fire and stand on his foot-sheet, wipe him dry with a clean cloth, and take him to bed to cure his troubles.

John Russell doesn't suggest that a wife should share her husband's bath, but this was an enjoyable, popular and economic alternative in the great wooden tubs of the time. The sponges were necessary as cushions to guard against splinters.

As you can see above, herbal rinses are used to keep skin and hair in good condition, but if you find you have to do a lot of dish-washing, laundry, scouring and scrubbing, you may require a moisturiser for your hands. Salves are the remedy for sore or dry skin. The name comes from the Latin *Salvia officinalis,* the sage plant, because a basic salve is made with sage and goose-grease. A common addition to the salve is marigold petals, reckoned to be especially good as hand cream.

If you work outdoors, I'm afraid there is no lotion with sun-protection factor 30. But sunburn shouldn't be a problem. Legs and arms are usually covered

A medieval bath (reconstruction).

by one layer of clothing at least, and sunhats, made of woven reeds or straw, are a must and readily available. When I spend time outside as a re-enactor, I find it's my neck that is most exposed because my hair is tucked inside my cap and the neckline of my gown is quite low at the back. However, a rectangle of linen, two corners tied in front and the rest of the cloth tucked into the back of my gown serves perfectly to prevent sunburn and is quite authentic as a medieval kerchief.

Chapter 5

Food and Shopping

What would I eat?

In medieval England you'll have to get used to a very different attitude to putting food on the table. In the twenty-first-century we go to the supermarket to buy whatever we fancy for breakfast, lunch, dinner, supper and snacks for at least a week at a time. If we have an allotment or garden, we may grow a few vegetables and fruits of our own or keep chickens for eggs, but otherwise we buy what we want. If you do have experience of growing your own, you'll be aware that things aren't always in season and back in medieval times this fact will seriously influence what you can eat and when. Also, people make do as far as possible with what they grow themselves and only shop for things they cannot produce at home.

Almost every dwelling comes with at least a small garden plot, even in crowded cities like London, and here the family try to grow as much as possible for their own use. If they manage to produce more than they need, the surplus will be sold or exchanged with a neighbour to add a bit of variety to the menu. The housewife is responsible for planting, weeding and tending the plot. She is also expected to know how to dry, salt, pickle and smoke just about anything to keep foodstuffs through the winter. Even so, there are times when the larder is looking very empty. In late spring and early summer the preserved food is almost gone and the new season's growth is only just beginning, so these are lean times for everyone but the wealthy.

All kinds of 'weeds' and wild plants can be made use of, so hedgerows, woodland and wayside can provide free ingredients, although it would be wise to make sure you know what is common land and which areas belong to the local lord, otherwise you could be in trouble.

Top tip

The tops of young stinging nettles can be cooked like spinach; older leaves can be used to dye linen a pretty green colour. The tough stems, dried and stripped, provide string.

Primrose and violet flowers are edible and can make a meal of the last of the winter preserves look more attractive. Daisies and violets are made into ointments to treat bruises. Wild garlic (or ramsons) blooms in April and May and its leaves and flowers are great for flavouring soups and sauces. Alexanders, not unlike celery, is another wayside plant that flowers early and can be eaten, although in medieval times it is specifically planted in gardens as a pot-herb. Other garden escapees have names like fat-hen and good-king-Henry and can go into the pot. In medieval England virtually every plant is useful.

Pot-herbs are any plant that is grown to be eaten, not just those we think of as herbs today. Cabbages (caboches), turnips, radishes and beetroot – whose leaves are eaten as well as the roots – parsnips, wild carrots and onions are pot-herbs, as well as sage, mint, parsley, sweet cicely, thyme and, after it is reintroduced in the fourteenth century, rosemary are what we today think of as herbs. Peas and beans are vital because they can be dried after harvesting and will keep for years, providing protein in the diet when there is no meat.

If you are poor, meat is going to be a rare luxury. Hard cheese – and I mean really *hard* cheese, made with skimmed milk – will be your protein, along with the pulses. These cheeses have to be softened by soaking before you can eat them. They can be kept on the rafters above the hearth where they are constantly smoked and last so long that they are sometimes bequeathed in wills to the next generation. Soft cheeses, like cream-cheese and cottage cheese, are meant for the rich man's table. Hopefully, you are a little more affluent and will have a more interesting diet.

As I mentioned in the introduction, many countryfolk and townsfolk keep a pig, buying it as a piglet in spring, feeding it on kitchen scraps throughout the summer, then sending it for slaughter in November. The meat is smoked as hams, salt-cured as bacon and salt pork, dried as the medieval equivalent of pork scratching, the odds and ends made into sausages and the blood into black pudding. Pigs' trotters are popular street food and the head is boiled, the meat removed and made into brawn to be served as the poorer man's version of the boar's head, a Christmas dinner centrepiece. Nothing is wasted. But so much pig meat might get tedious and many households sell parts of their pig and use the money to buy other things.

Staple foods – bread and ale

One vital commodity everyone needs is grain. On more fertile soils, wheat and barley are grown; on poorer soils, oats and rye. All four kinds of grain are milled into flour for making bread, an everyday staple. Barley is also malted and brewed into ale. Oats are the basic ingredient of pottage: a thick porridge-type stew into which any herbs, vegetables, meat or fish can be added. Similarly, instead of oats, wheat can be used, in which case the dish is called frumenty. Rye bread is dark in colour and not so popular but rye flour mixed with wheat flour is more acceptable for every day. Pure white wheaten bread used to be for their lordships only, but by the fifteenth century everybody wants white bread.

DID YOU KNOW?

Common folk complained about not getting white bread because the lords ate it all. Their lordships argued that working folk needed to eat wholegrain brown bread and lords could not because wholegrain makes you fart and that's just not polite in high society.

You will have bread with every meal and though it's tempting to think that it will be home-baked and fresh from the oven, that may not be possible; even getting the flour and yeast to make the dough may not be straightforward. To turn the grain into flour, it must be milled. In the countryside, people often grind their own, using quern stones, though some lords of the manor own mills (as mentioned in Chapter 2). Here, both the lord and the miller take a cut of the profits, usually in terms of a proportion of the tenants' flour once it's milled. You can see why this is unpopular. Also, millers are, by tradition at least, always greedy and conniving characters, taking more than their due share.

Once you have your grain milled, or purchased ready-ground from a market, all you require is water to make a dough, adding a dash of salt and any flavourings. When your dough is made, you can shape it into little round cakes and bake it on a hot hearth stone to make flat-bread, oat-cakes, or whatever. For poorer folk, this is their daily staple. But you may prefer bread made with a raising agent. Yeast is the most traditional and still in use in the twenty-first century for most breads, except types such as soda bread or sour-dour bread which are a bit different. Yeast is most easily come by as an incidental by-product of brewing ale. As the ale ferments, a frothy scum forms on top of the liquor. This is 'barm' and it contains enough yeast to add to your dough or to set up the next brewing of ale.

The experienced medieval baker knows how much kneading is required and how long the dough needs to be left to rise before a final kneading into shape, ready for baking. Small loaves – like our modern rolls – can be baked individually on a hot hearth stone if they're covered by an earthen pot to form a kind of mini-oven, but for a full-sized family or household loaf this won't work because the dough in the centre will not be cooked. You need a 'proper' oven.

A medieval bread oven.

Medieval ovens like this one don't come with instructions. Like all other cookery procedures, experience is the best teacher. The oven is heated before any food is cooked by lighting a fire inside and leaving it to heat up while the dough – or pies or whatever – is prepared. Once your experience says the oven is up to temperature – apparently, how close you can stand to the opening is quite an accurate guide – you rake out the hot ashes and put in your bread. A wooden door closes in the heat and is sealed around the edges with oddments of dough. When these dry out and fall off, the bread inside should be ready. Having removed the bread, don't waste the heat. Pies go in next, followed by small cakes. Even then, once those are baked, the oven is still hot enough to dry herbs or even to kill off parasites in chicken feathers before you use them to stuff pillows.

Your bread will probably be blackened on the bottom with ash from the fire. You can dust it off but, if it's going to be served to important people, you'll have to trim off the sooty base. That's why posh folk are known as the 'upper crust' because only common folk eat the bottom of a loaf.

As you can see, baking is a complex business and raking out the burning ashes is particularly dangerous. So dangerous, in fact, that in some towns and cities, like London, where houses are close together, private dwellings are forbidden to have ovens because of the obvious risk of fire and the chance of it spreading to other buildings.

Because of the hazards, only proper bakeries are allowed to have ovens and this trade is often located outside the city. When your homemade dough is ready, you take it to the baker, who will put it in his oven alongside other people's dough. By tradition every household has a design or letter to mark the loaves as theirs, and the old nursery rhyme 'Pat-a-cake, Pat-a-cake, baker's man' refers to this:

> Pat-a-cake, Pat-a-cake, baker's man,
> Bake me a cake as fast as you can.
> Prick it and pat it and mark it with 'B'
> And put it in the oven for Baby and me.

Bakers will also cook pies, biscuits and cakes for you, but beware of malpractice. A group of London bakers were taken to court after it was discovered their kneading tables were fitted with tiny trap-doors.

Even as the customer watched the baker give his bread a final knead, an apprentice, hidden under the table, opened the trap-door and stole a lump of the dough. Eventually, the baker would have enough stolen dough to make a free batch of loaves. Not only were the bakers prosecuted; the carpenters who made the tables were fined as well.

If you don't make your own dough, you can still buy your bread from a baker, but again, watch out. A group of baxters (female bakers) were fined for selling underweight loaves. Smaller loaves are bought by the dozen, and these women were required, from henceforth, to sell thirteen for the price of twelve, to ensure the customer got value for money. 'Thirteen' is still known as 'a baker's dozen'. Another ploy used by disreputable bakers is to poke bits of metal into their bread to make sure it's heavy enough to pass any on-the-spot checks carried out under the Assize of Bread act, which determines the standards of bread sold to the public throughout England. It's not unknown for bakers to adulterate their flour either, perhaps with ground acorns or beans, or even chalk powder. It will be to your advantage to get to know your local bakers; which are trustworthy and bake the best bread.

Grain, usually barley, is also used to brew ale. In medieval England, brewing is another job for women, done on a domestic scale. (This remains the case until Tudor times, when hops are added to ale to make beer as they act as a preservative and allow the beer to keep much longer. Therefore, it becomes possible to brew on an industrial scale and men tend to take over the process. Hops, however, have a bitter flavour and the new drink takes a while to catch on.) Even home brewing requires quite a bit of equipment that not every household can afford or has the space to store. It also needs a good fire to be kept burning, so the cost of fuel is another expense. For these reasons, in London at least, it is often the wives of well-to-do merchants who take up brewing to earn 'pin money' for themselves. Any ale surplus to household requirements can be sold to the public, once the local ale-taster or ale-conner has tried it for quality and checked out the measures, according to the Assize of Ale act. This means ale-houses are often of the pop-up type – here today and gone tomorrow – until the next batch is brewed.

As with bread, until you learn how to make your own ale from an expert – if you want to go to so much effort – it will be as well to get to know the local brewsters. Everyone will likely have a slightly different recipe, perhaps adding sweet herbs in season or spices for a special occasion, such as Christmas, and you're bound to develop a preference. And like the bakers, some brewsters are more reliable than others.

How would I cook the food?

Most medieval cooking methods will be familiar to you: frying, boiling, baking, stewing, roasting and toasting. Broiling and seething just mean boiling or simmering. Quite often, meat or vegetables will be cooked twice, parboiled before being fried or baked. All food should be over cooked, rather than under done, and never ever *al dente*. Fresh fruit is regarded with suspicion by the medical profession so you are advised to cook fruit, not to eat it straight off the tree or bush. Remember too, some familiar foodstuffs of the twenty-first century, especially those from the Americas, don't exist in medieval cuisine. They include potatoes and sweet potatoes, tomatoes, sweet peppers and chillies, sweetcorn, avocados and – very sadly – chocolate. No matter, you'll have the joy of trying blaunderelles, chibols and lampreys.[1]

Towards the end of the medieval period, recipes (called 'receipts') start to be written down and shared, though measurements and cooking times are rarely given. The reasons for this are that weighing things out in pounds and ounces isn't possible for the average cook without weighing scales. Flour is bought by the sackful, milk by the jug and butter by the pat. Only goldsmiths weigh tiny amounts. Everything is judged by eye and experience counts. The same with cooking times. Whether baking in an oven or over an open hearth, there are no thermometers; you just have to test the food to see when it's cooked. Sadly, since most poorer folk can't read or write, recipes are pointless to them so all the cookery notes that have survived are for the better off who could read them. Here is a recipe for blancmange but don't expect a sweet standing custard. It means 'white food' and is a posh recipe using the luxuries of tender chicken, rice, almonds and even sugar.

> Take two parts [long grain] rice and one part [ground] almonds. Wash the rice in lukewarm water then boil it in chicken stock until almost tender. Use more chicken stock to steep the almonds until you get almond 'milk'.

Drain the rice and leave to cool. Take cooked white chicken meat and chop small. Strain the almond milk, add the rice and heat until not quite boiling. Add the chicken meat and a little melted chicken fat to make a richer dish and thicken the sauce. Season with salt, pepper if you can afford it and serve the dish decorated with flaked almonds, toasted. Sprinkle with a little fine sugar.[2]

The addition of sugar may surprise you but medieval people have no hesitation in mixing sweet with savoury, and sugar and spices are symbols of affluence, so are used at every opportunity.

The recipe above pales into insignificance when we look at the shopping list for a feast given by King Richard II and his uncle, John of Gaunt, Duke of Lancaster, on 23 September 1387. The list of meat and poultry is astounding: 16 oxen and 14 veal calves; 120 sheep; 12 boars and 140 pigs; 3 ton & 3 does of venison (not sure what these measurements mean); 50 swans; 210 geese; more than 1,000 chickens of various kinds; 6 kid goats; nearly 500 rabbits; 1,200 pigeons; plus pheasants, herons, bittern; 144 curlews; 144 partridges; 12 cranes and 'enough' wild fowl (ducks of various species); 120 gallons of milk; 12 gallons of cream; 11 gallons of curds (like soft cheese); 12 bushels of apples and ... 11,000 eggs.

What a feast that must have been, but we don't know how many were coming to eat. So let's talk to King Richard's master cook about his work:

> Good Sir Cook, we read your shopping list for yesterday's feast with great interest. Can you tell us about your work in the royal kitchens?
>
> Work? Cookery is a fine craft, an art. It takes skill and finesse. I'm not some clod-hopping labourer, I'll have you know.
>
> But someone must peel the onions and scour the pots.
>
> We have scullions to do those tasks. I'm the creator of masterpieces. For yesterday's feast, I constructed a castle, nigh as tall as a man, complete with battlements, drawbridge and smoking cannon. What a wonder it was too. Even the Duke of Lancaster remarked upon it. Did you see it?

No. I wasn't invited. But I want to hear more about this great castle. How did you make it?

I made it out of four separate pies, all different. A large square pork pie stood in the centre, the pastry coloured yellow with saffron. That was the castle keep. Another was a sweet pie, round in shape, made with almonds and coloured red with sanders.

You mean sandalwood?

That's what I said. Another was a round fruit pie with figs, raisons, apples and pears, browned in the oven. The fourth pie was made of sweet almond fritters stacked high and coloured green with parsley juice. I arranged these three as towers around the keep.

Why not four towers?

Don't you know anything, you buffoon? Three in honour of the Holy Trinity, of course.

Oh, I see. Then what about the battlements and drawbridge?

All modelled from salt-crust pastry, baked hard and then coloured, as with the pies. Then I glued them together with a wash of ayren.

Ayren?

Eggs. We folk from Kent call them ayren.

And what about the cannon, Sir Cook? How did you make them?

Ah! That's my secret but I will tell you this: I put real gunpowder inside them. Now, clear off. I have a peacock to dress back in its feathered finery and my marvellous cockatrice to put together.

What's a cockatrice, sir?

Out! I can't have you under my feet in my kitchen when I'm working miracles. Go away before I beat you with my trusty ladle, you idle rascal.[3]

A cockatrice, or cokentrice, if you should meet one, comes in two forms: the front half of a cockerel stitched to the back half of a piglet, or the piglet's front end sewn to the cockerel's tail end. They're then roasted on a spit. Towards the end of cooking, they are washed with egg

A cross-looking cook wields a meat cleaver.

yolk dyed with any of the food colourings Sir Cook mentioned above: saffron yellow, sanders red and parsley green, or for a truly royal dish imperial purple using a plant called turnsole. Or real gold leaf can be stuck on the cockatrice with egg wash as an extra decoration and is also popular as a coating for posh meatballs. Gold leaf can be eaten and passes through the body unchanged. People known as scawagers earn a living from emptying latrine pits and going through the poo to recover any gold leaf is one of the perks of the job.

DID YOU KNOW?

Medieval pastry isn't usually meant to be eaten. Like the castle battlements above, the pie crust is made with a half flour/half salt mixture. It becomes a solid container for the filling. When baked, the lid of the pie is lifted off, the contents dished out and the pastry discarded, being inedible.

How would I buy food and goods?

For any foodstuffs you cannot grow or produce from your garden plot, you will have to go a-marketing; i.e., shopping. In early medieval times there are no shops. Every commodity is sold from temporary stalls set up in the market place, or even from trays slung around the neck or carried on the head of the salesperson. These mobile vendors are called hucksters and are not always the most trustworthy, as shown by the numerous occasions when they are brought before the Courts of Piepowder (see Chapter 10). Markets are often weekly or twice weekly events, but laws exist to make sure each town in a particular area holds its market on a different day of the week and, except in remote parts, that markets are about eight miles apart. The idea is that a sixteen-mile walk, there and back, to sell your produce and buy what you need, is perfectly possible during daylight hours. I did say you have to be fit.

Also, at these early markets, bartering goods is normal. You can exchange your dozen eggs from your hens, bunches of herbs or surplus worts from your garden for a square of leather to mend your shoe, a new horn spoon or a round of cheese. Money replaces bartering only gradually and specialist shops come into existence quite late in the medieval period. Some of the first food shops, as we would recognise them, sell dairy produce and strict regulations state how things should be displayed separately so flavours aren't transferred, in particular from cheese to butter. In fifteenth-century London, dairy produce is sold from stalls set up in the nave of St Paul's Cathedral because the old stone building is always cool, even in summer, so the butter doesn't melt and milk and cream keep better.

As well as avoiding suspect bakers and brewers, you will have to beware of people known as forestallers and regrators. Edmund Cadon, a cook, appeared in the Lord Mayor's Court in London on 1 December 1366. He was accused of having bought geese at Leadenhall Market the previous Sunday before the hour of Prime, which was against the custom or regulation of the city. He was sent to prison.[4] His crime is an example of 'forestalling', that is buying goods before the market opens for business officially; in this case, when the church bells ring for Prime, the first hour of the day, at 6am.

On 30 January 1374 the same court tried John Wastel, a poulterer, who purchased poultry from 'foreign' poulterers, i.e., from outside London, before they reached Billingsgate Market 'in order to forestall it'. He had bought 6 curlews, 1 mallard, 12 teals and '10 sticks with 22 birds' (The sticks were a means of carrying ducks and chickens by tying their feet to the sticks so their heads hung down.) John forfeited all the birds and was committed to prison until he paid their value of six shillings plus half a mark fine (6s 8d). He paid up the same day and was released.[5]

Regrators are worse. They buy up goods from more reputable traders, such as bread that wouldn't pass the assize, or fish that's hardly fit to eat, getting it very cheaply. They then sell the goods at just a fraction below the full price, attracting poorer customers who can't afford to pay for the best, but they get substandard produce which may even be dangerous to eat.

Some of the first traders to open proper shops in larger towns are the pepperers, later called grocers. Their guilds or fellowships are set up early. The Guild of Pepperers was set up in London in 1180, becoming the Worshipful Company of Grocers in 1345. 'Pepperers' are

A medieval market.

so called because pepper is one of their most profitable and important commodities. 'Grocers' or 'grossores' describes how they run their businesses: buying stuff *en gros* or in bulk, wholesale, then weighing it out into amounts suitable for retail to customers. Their range of goods is surprising, as we see from the Countess of Leicester's discussion of her shopping list in Chapter 2. Spices from the Orient, sugar, rice and almonds are some of the luxury goods they sell, but grocers also import dry food stuffs such as raisins and currants, figs, dates and cherries, as well as inedible things like dyes and pigments or even medicinal ingredients.

If you don't have time to cook a meal or get hungry while out marketing, by the fifteenth century most towns have at least one or two cookshops, where you can buy a meal ready made, either to eat in the shop or take away. Here is part of a poem copied out by John Lydgate in the fifteenth century called *London Lickpenny*. The poem tells of a poor lad who comes to Westminster from the Kent countryside, hoping to bring his law case to court. He soon discovers you can't do anything in the city without money. These stanzas tell what happens when its dinnertime:

> Then to Westminster Gate I presently went,
> When the sun was at highe prime;
> Cooks to me they took good intent,
> And proffered me bread with ale and wine,
> Ribs of beef, both fat and full fine;
> A fair cloth they gan for to sprede,
> But wanting Money I might not then speed.
>
> Then unto London I did me hie,
> Of all the land it beareth the prize.
> "Hot peascods!" one began to cry, [pea pods, like mange tout]
> "Strawberry ripe!" and "Cherries in the rise!"
> One bade me come near and buy some spice,
> Pepper and saffron they gan me bede,
> But for lack of Money I might not speed.

Eating out is possible in medieval towns, so long as you can afford it, but it seems to have been done only when necessary, not for a pleasurable romantic evening out.

Money, weights and measures

Monetary accounts are calculated in pounds, shillings and pence (12 pence = a shilling; and 20 shillings = a pound), although, surprisingly, there aren't any actual coins equal to pounds and shillings until Henry VII's reign when, in 1489, the first gold piece worth 20s (£1) is minted and called a sovereign. Medieval people use coins of values we don't recognise today: marks. Marks are worth 13 shillings and 4 pence. A gold coin called a noble, invented in the reign of Edward III, is worth 6s 8d, so it's half a mark or one-third of £1. It's the highest value coin in England (and probably in Europe) until 1464 when, in the reign of Edward IV, the gold noble becomes the rose-noble, or ryal, and is now valued at 10s, although the weight doesn't increase significantly. At the same time, another gold coin of lesser weight is issued, known as the angel because the obverse side bears an image of the Archangel St Michael slaying the dragon of evil. This becomes the coin worth 6s 8d, and there are also a gold half-angel worth 3s 4d and a quarter-angel worth 1s 8d.

As a humble citizen, it will be a rare thing if you ever see one of these gold coins. Your purse will likely hold silver groats, worth 4 pence, which can be cut in halves or even quarters to produce pieces valued at 2d x 2 or 1d x 4. Most common are the silver pennies, which can also be cut in half to give halfpennies or into 'fourthings', or farthings as they were known, worth a quarter of a penny. Silver coins often bear a cross-shape so they can be cut accurately. The silver coins carry the head of a king, a general design introduced by Edward I in 1279, which survives until the Tudor period.

Weights and measures are confusing even for those who are born in medieval times, so for you they will be difficult to understand. This is a legal statute issued in the fourteenth century: 'An English penny shall weigh 32 wheat grains from the middle of the ear and an ounce shall weigh 20 pence. And 12 ounces make a London pound and 8 pounds make a gallon of wine and 8 gallons of wine make a London bushel.' Confused? You're not the only one.

Some commodities appear to be described rather than measured. So salmon could be bought 'as thick as a man's arm', or wood 'as much as a man can carry', and hay and straw 'as much as a man can lift'. In London, cloth can be bought by the yard and handful, the extra bit ensuring the draper or mercer doesn't sell his customer a short yard with the possibility of prosecution. London's famous St Bartholomew's Fair, held every August since 1133, was originally a cloth fair. By the 1400s it is the place to buy anything you can think of: glassware, leather goods, exotic pets like monkeys and popinjays – parrots – or even scientific instruments such as astrolabes. But the fair still opens with the presentation of the Merchant-Tailors' official silver yardstick against which every yard measure to be used during the fair has to be checked.

Perhaps one of the trickiest things to buy is coal, which can be sold by the seam, the horse-load, the load, the corf, the perch, the fother, the cauldron or chauldron, the keep or the barge-load.[6] If you manage to sort that out while you're back in medieval England, please explain it to the rest of us when you come home.

Chapter 6

Health and Medicine

England in the Middle Ages is not always a healthy place. Particularly in the crowded, unhygienic towns and cities, epidemic diseases are a fact of life, but out in the countryside the air is clean and pollution usually concerns a neighbour's livestock stirring up the water and urinating in the river, or the washerwoman's soap tainting the stream. However, you will likely have to be aware of other health issues almost unknown in the twenty-first century. There are no insecticides, fungicides, weed-killers or artificial fertilisers sprayed on the crops, which sounds like the healthy option until you realise what that means for your diet. There is likely no such thing as an unblemished apple or spinach leaves without holes chewed by insects. Mould – a fungus – can be a serious hazard. Ergot is a mould which can grow on rye in a damp season. Eating bread made with infected rye may cause hallucinations and a kind of mad hysteria. If an entire village is affected it's a serious matter.

Poisonous weeds may be harvested along with any crops and any produce is likely to be smaller and less nutritious because manure – the only fertiliser – is in short supply, often reserved for his lordship's fields. So human waste serves to nourish your garden plot or field strips and here is another cause of health problems: parasites. The eggs of various human gut parasites, such as tapeworms and roundworms, are passed out with the faeces and survive in the soil. Any crops not scrupulously washed before eating may have eggs on them and pass on to infect a new host.

DID YOU KNOW?

Even the most noble aren't immune to gut parasites: when the skeleton of King Richard III was discovered by archaeologists in Leicester in 2012, evidence of a serious infection of roundworms was found where his intestines would have been.

Other more familiar parasites – fleas, lice and bedbugs – are very common, but medieval folk know which herbs can keep them under control to some extent. Fleabane, lavender and lady's bedstraw can all help, using them in the mattress stuffing, strewing them on the floor or tucking them into your clothing. If you haven't taken a course of anti-malaria pills before you journey back in time, lavender water can deter mosquitoes. This is vital in marshy areas of southern England where these irritating insects flourish and can carry malaria, although medieval folk call this disease in its various forms 'the ague'.

Apart from the problem of parasitic diseases, you are probably most at risk from death by accident. This could be as dramatic as a mishap with a scythe at harvest time, severing some vital part, or it may be something minor, like a splinter in the thumb. Without any scientific knowledge of antibiotics, any injury, however small, can result in infection, sepsis and possibly death. But take heart: all is not lost. Just because medieval folk have never heard of antibiotics doesn't mean they don't have them. Wounds are washed with wine, if available, red for preference. Red wine, being a dark red liquid, is believed to 'inspire' the body to produce more blood to replace what has been lost, and also happens to be a good antiseptic.

Surgeons know how to pack open wounds so that they heal from the inside out, using sphagnum moss or cobwebs, both of which have antibiotic properties. Surgeons are skilled at stitching and cauterising wounds too. Cobwebs can also be used to staunch bleeding, helping the blood to clot and form a scab. Various remedies make use of vinegar being left to stand in a brass pot for some days. Vinegar reacts with copper in the brass to produce copper salts, another good antibiotic. Honey, smeared onto any wound, acts as a seal, as well as an antibiotic and antiviral healing agent.

Perhaps one of the best treatments of this kind – though expensive – is dragon's blood. This may sound like something from a fairytale, but it does exist. It has nothing to do with dragons but is a red tree resin, although the legend lives on in that the tree is called *Draconis*. Various of the species grow in the Far East, but medieval folk import the resin from the Canary Islands. It can be used as a dye for textiles, a paint pigment and a throat medicine. If a *Draconis* tree is damaged it oozes a bright red sap, a liquid resin that looks like blood. The resin sets hard, forming a shield over the damaged area to protect it while it heals, but it also contains antibiotic, antiviral and anti-inflammatory properties to promote healing. A paste is made with the powdered resin which can be smeared over an injury to do for humans what it does for the tree.

Top tip

A quick and soothing treatment for small burns is to find a snail and rub its slime on the burn. Slime protects the snail from injury and helps heal any nicks and cuts it suffers. It can do the same for people.

What diseases will you be most vulnerable to?

Living in a town, where folk are more crowded together, epidemics are unavoidable. Typhoid fever, typhus, dysentery, measles, scarlet fever, diphtheria and smallpox are just some of the afflictions that snatch away lives in alarming numbers. Most feared of all, after its first visitation to England in 1348, is the plague. These diseases have no respect for rank; a king is as susceptible as a commoner but at least – you might think – royalty can afford to take countermeasures. Even in the thirteenth century, the connection between dirt and disease is understood, although it's described in terms of 'foul airs' rather than bacteria and viruses, so a clean house is a healthy house. The rich can travel to their other residences while servants scrub and refresh the place they've left. For the poor, however, this isn't an option when disease appears in the vicinity.

There are two schools of thought on what to do when plague breaks out: pray hard, avoid sin and be virtuous, so God might see fit to spare you; or enjoy life to the full while you can.

Top tip

Knowing the plague is passed on by flea-bites, you can be generous with the insect repellents, lavender and fleabane and encourage your friends to do the same.

The first cases of plague among the 100,000 population of London occurred in early October 1348. Perhaps it's no surprise that John de Foxton, the deputy coroner, was among them, yet King Edward III was frequently in the capital and at nearby Westminster (which remained plague-free for the present) during October, November and December. Although his own daughter, Joan, had recently died of plague on her way to Spain to marry King Pedro, far from isolating himself in a country retreat, Edward held splendid tournaments at Windsor, Reading, Eltham, Canterbury, Bury and Lichfield, inviting all the nobility. It seems he was one of the 'eat, drink and be merry ...' faction, who saw little point in excessive religious fervour and abstemious living in the hope God would keep them safe. And no wonder when so many churchmen were rapidly succumbing. When the Archbishop of Canterbury died in August 1348 – not from plague – the king wanted his Chancellor, John Ufford, to replace him.

Duly appointed, the new archbishop continued his work as Chancellor at Westminster, but in the spring of 1349 the seat of government, as yet unscathed despite its proximity to plague-ridden London, had its first casualties among the law clerks. The king's physician who attended them soon fell sick and died too, followed on 20 May by the Chancellor himself, before he was even consecrated as archbishop. This time the king did retire to Woodstock in Oxfordshire and the law courts were closed from 15 June to 14 July, but Edward was back at Westminster in August. During that month, he welcomed Ufford's replacement as Archbishop of Canterbury, Thomas Bradwardine, at Eltham Palace in Kent. Bradwardine had just returned from Avignon in France, where the Pope had confirmed him in office, and swiftly moved on to London. However, during the short journey from Eltham, the new archbishop also became ill. Four days later, he too died of plague, having caught it in France. As you can see, no one is safe from this scourge.

How healthy would I be?

You may be one of the lucky ones who avoid catching plague. It is a fact that fleas find some folk tastier than others so they may not like you. Also, having arrived as a well-nourished, healthy visitor from the twenty-first century, you will have a better chance than most of surviving, if you do catch it. As with many diseases, once you've had it, you'll be immune to it in future. That's why, during the subsequent plague epidemic of 1361, it seemed to kill far more children because many adults, having lived through the first visitation, had either developed immunity to it or were the ones the fleas didn't fancy for breakfast.

However healthy and fit you are, we can all suffer from colds, headaches, sore throats, upset stomachs, skin rashes and any number of minor ailments, so you'll want to know what treatments are available, if any. If you live in a small community in the countryside, the village wise-woman is probably the best source of advice and a remedy. She will know which plants can aid which ailments and brew a 'simple' for you. A simple consists of a single ingredient, boiled up in water to be drunk like tea, or perhaps pounded in goose grease to be applied as an ointment or even hung around your neck to ward off anything nasty, or attract a lover. Some of the wise-woman's treatments smack of witch's spells and good luck charms but others really can work.

For example, a plant called meadowsweet grows in damp places across England. Rarer now, it's common in medieval times and has many uses. It has creamy white flowers in high summer, smelling of honey and beloved by bees. The whole plant has a pleasant, fresh smell and is popular as a strewing herb to put down on the floor as a perfumed carpet and insect trap. Most useful of all, meadowsweet contains an active aspirin derivative. It can cure a headache, bring down fever and reduce swelling, but unlike aspirin proper, it soothes rather than irritates the stomach lining so is also good for stomach upsets.

If you live in a town, you should get to know your

Meadowsweet – good for fevers, headaches and pain relief.

77

local apothecary – the medieval pharmacist – in case you have need of a remedy. He can also supply you with a simple, but since he has access to a host of more exotic ingredients, he will likely persuade you to try a remedy with multiple contents. Some may work, while others could do more harm than good. Spices like cinnamon, ginger and aniseed, or herbs like fennel and dill can all calm an upset stomach. Betony and valerian help headaches and act as a tonic, but don't let him add foxglove (digitalis), monkshood (aconite) or deadly nightshade (belladonna) to your medicine since they're likely to prove fatal. The apothecary knows that, but for some stubborn ailments it's thought anything is worth a try. Other remedies are just – well – weird. Here's one for treating a serious throat infection, known as quinsy. It's probably best to avoid this, if only for the sake of the animals involved: 'For him that has a quinsy. Take a fat cat and flay it well. Clean and draw out the guts. Take the grease of a hedgehog and the fat of a bear and resins and fenugreek and sage and gum of honeysuckle and virgin wax. All this crumble small and stuff the cat within as you would a goose. Roast it all and gather the grease and anoint him [the patient] with it.'[1]

Supposing the worst befalls you and you need surgery? Surgeons are perfectly capable of dealing with nose polyps and cataracts, haemorrhoids and splinting a broken bone, but these procedures hurt. There were no medieval anaesthetics, right? Wrong. If both you and the surgeon are willing to take the risk, there is a mixture dating back to Anglo-Saxon times, and still in use, that can put you to sleep during surgery: dwale. Here is a fourteenth-century recipe for this potent sleeping draught: 'To make a drink that men call dwale, to make a man [or woman] sleep during an operation. Take the gall of a boar, three spoonfuls of the juice of hemlock and three spoonfuls of wild bryony, lettuce, opium poppy, henbane and vinegar. Mix them well together and then let the man [or woman] sit by a good fire and make him/her drink of the potion until he/she falls asleep. Then he/she may safely be operated upon.'

The problem here is the possibility of putting the patient to sleep forever with poisonous hemlock, henbane and opium. Even lettuce is a soporific. The saving grace is the wild bryony, which has a rapid laxative effect, passing the potion through the patient's digestive system so quickly that the lethal ingredients don't have time to take their full toxic effect.

DID YOU KNOW?

There seems to be an idea that surgeons got their patients drunk so they wouldn't feel pain during an operation. Not true. Medieval surgeons were aware that alcohol thins the blood, making it more likely the patient would bleed to death.

What is my life expectancy?

If you survive or manage to avoid all those deadly diseases, fatal accidents and the traumas of surgery – with or without anaesthetic – you have a very reasonable chance of living into your eighties. This may sound surprising, and if you consult any tables about life expectancy in medieval England before you travel back, seem unlikely, but it's true. The trouble is that infant death is a common occurrence, a sadness experienced time and again by some families. But if a child lives to be a teenager, life expectancy increases significantly. Since you have, most likely, already left your childhood behind, you have overcome the biggest hurdle.

For those in early adulthood, the life-threatening dangers become different for men and women. For men, the greatest risks lie in warfare, fighting and perilous work, such as tiling or thatching roofs, cutting timber, hunting, fishing or dealing with heavy animals such as oxen and horses. For women, childbirth is always dangerous; before, during and after delivery. That is why many of the most long-lived folk are churchmen, who neither labour nor fight, or nuns, who never have babies. Thomas Bourchier, Cardinal Archbishop of Canterbury, had a long life, though his precise date of birth isn't known. It varies from 1404 to 1412, depending on the source of information, but since he lived until 1486, he did rather well. However, it isn't always the case that you have to be in the Church to live beyond your biblical three-score-years-and-ten.

Cecily Neville, Dowager Duchess of York, was born on 3 May in 1415, the year of the battle of Agincourt, and died on 31 May in 1495, having just had her eightieth birthday. Although Proud Cis, as she was known, did take a vow of chastity after her husband, Richard,

79

Duke of York, was killed at the battle of Wakefield in December 1460, she had certainly done her duty, producing children, as the following anonymous contemporary poem records:

> Sir, aftir the tyme of long bareynesse
> God first sent Anne, which signyfieth grace,
> In token that al her hertis hevynesse
> He, as for bareynesse, wold fro hem chace.
> Harry, Edward and Edmonde, each in his place
> Succeeded, and aftir tweyn doughtris came,
> Elizabeth and Margarete, and afterward William.
>
> John aftir William nexte borne was,
> Which bothe be passid to Godis grace.
> George was nexte, and aftir Thomas
> Borne was, which sone aftir did pace
> By the path of dethe to the hevenly place.
> Richard liveth yit; but the last of alle
> Was Ursula, to Hym whom God list calle.[2]

This poem starkly tells us of the loss of so many children and the numerous pregnancies and confinements Cecily survived. She must have been tough. Her 'long barrenness' mentioned at the beginning was most likely because the duke and duchess were married as children, but once old enough to consummate the union, Cecily bore twelve children. Anne became Duchess of Exeter, Elizabeth became Duchess of Suffolk and Margaret became Duchess of Burgundy; of the daughters, only Ursula, the last born, died in infancy. Of the sons, Henry, William, John and Thomas died as babies, but Edward became Earl of March and then King Edward IV; Edmund became Earl of Rutland, but died at the battle of Wakefield as a teenager, beside his father; George became Duke of Clarence and Richard became Duke of Gloucester and later King Richard III. Cecily, as a royal duchess, must have had the best maternity care available but only seven of her dozen children lived to grow up. That's over fifty per cent success rate and better than many families, rich and poor, could manage.

How useful are physicians?

From the twelfth century onwards, physicians are university trained but medical schools are rare and students very few. It takes seven years to qualify and 'drop-outs' are more common than those who get their doctorate.

Oxford University began c.1167 and Cambridge University was set up in 1209 by students fleeing from Oxford after one of their number was murdered. There are never more than a handful of medical students at either and Englishmen (never women, I'm afraid) tend to go abroad to complete their medical training. At Bologna – one of the most advanced medical schools – an average of just four physicians qualify each year in the fifteenth century.

Students attend lectures and read a set list of books, most of which date back to Ancient Greece and Rome. They are expected to memorise chapter after chapter of writing by Hippocrates, Galen (who had been the doctor to emperors and gladiators) and Aristotle and never question these ancient authorities. Examinations are always *viva voce,* one-to-one with the examiner and no writing down of answers required.

DID YOU KNOW?

In 1278 the Englishman Roger Bacon dared suggest the physicians should do their research instead of relying on old texts alone. The church authorities threw him in prison for having such outrageous ideas.

Despite their knowledge being derived from such old sources, it isn't all bad. Holistic medicine is the thing: treating the body as a whole, not just the obvious symptoms. This means the basic treatments involve diet, exercise, sleep, bathing or simply opening or closing particular windows. Good health requires your bodily humours – blood, phlegm, yellow bile and black bile – to be in balance. An excess of cold, damp phlegm can be balanced by eating spicy, drying beef; too much fiery black bile can be countered by cold, wet fish. Too much exercise, sleep or even sex can be as bad as too little; 'moderation' is the rule. Bathing is soothing and good for certain skin problems, but is also counted as the 'opposite' of exercise. Certain weather conditions are believed to affect the balance of the humours: winter weather often heralds colds (an excess of phlegm), so it makes sense to close the window on chill, damp winds. Hot summers see an increase in fevers, so opening a window to cooler airs is advised.

Physicians are required to study the stars and be able to draw up horoscopes. In medieval England, it's believed the stars, under God's guiding hand, control and predict what happens on earth. A doctor needs to know in advance whether a patient is likely to recover or not before beginning any treatment. Firstly, this is so that he can advise the patient to write his will, set his affairs in order and prepare his soul, if death is the likely outcome. Secondly, if recovery isn't expected, no sensible physician will give treatment for fear of being blamed when the patient dies. A doctor relies on having a good reputation and lawsuits for malpractice aren't unknown. And thirdly, if the stars foretell a good recovery, then the physician has everything to gain by giving the correct diagnosis and treatment and taking the credit for the patient's return to good health.

As we've seen, however, even by the fifteenth century university-qualified physicians are rare, so their services don't come cheap, though there are alternatives. Let's talk to John Crophill about his work in Essex:

> Good day, Master Crophill. You treat patients for miles around but you never went to university. How did you train as a physician?
>
> The priest in our village taught me to read and write and I was always interested in medicine. These days, it's easy enough to find medical works written in English with everything a physician needs to know. I taught myself. No need for the expense and waste of years at university when it's all there, in a book.
>
> Tell us what you learned from your studies that has been of most use.
>
> I've written the important bits in my notebook, details of bloodletting; the zodiac; the planets' influences and

effect throughout the year on the four humours and bodily parts; on the moon; the seven ages of man; the study of urine, diet and treatment according to the months and an excellent treatise on calculations to know what thou wilt. That treatise has been of great help. I used it to find a lost rosary for the Prioress of Wix, told Will the Shearman the best day to wed Joan and correctly predicted that Thomas Gale's wife would have a son, at last. I've also noted some good remedies for gout and warts.

But I've heard that medicine isn't your main employment.

No, it's not. I serve as bailiff of Wix Priory, a small house of Benedictine nuns here in Essex, since 1455. I earn more from that than I ever could as a physician. For my duties of rent collecting and court attendances as the manor bailiff, I get about 40s a year – that's a goodly sum. And some years I've been paid as the local ale-taster, checking quality and measures of ale sold by local tavern-keepers and housewives. I also have medical duties at the priory but that doesn't take much trouble, for though the house is wealthy, there are only three nuns and the prioress.

How do you fit in your duties and your medical work?

As I travel around, collecting the rents due, I treat anyone in need of my services as a physician as well.

Tell us about some of your patients.

What! You've never heard that what passes betwixt patient and physician is like unto a confession made to a priest? We never tell.

Oh. Well, can you tell us what you charge for your treatments?

Aye, I suppose that'll do no harm but what I ask depends on the patient's wealth. I charged Richard Armystyd 6s 8d, because he can afford it, for a gout remedy made with ground elder – works well, that does – but I only charged William Fortlie tuppence for the same. For treating the wife of John Armystyd in Otley, I charged 13s 4d for medications when she suffered inflammation of the lungs, him being rich. But Hob the Herdsmen I treated for free when he was afflicted likewise. That's how it works, see: I charge the wealthy so I can treat the poor for nothing. That's the Christian way. And look! I've told of my patients' secrets. You tricked me.

Apologies, Master Crophill.[3]

One disease few are troubled by in the twenty-first century is of great concern in medieval times: leprosy. Although we know leprosy isn't particularly contagious and is treatable with today's medicines, in those days it was a terrible affliction and seen as a kind of living death. Lazar-houses are founded all over Europe, where lepers can be accommodated away from healthy folk. Leprosy is an unclean contamination to be avoided at all costs.

However, by 1350s leprosy is dying out in England – no one knows why – but of course it's replaced by the deadly plague. Lazar-houses are often converted into pest-houses in an effort to quarantine the new disease. But leprosy, though now rare, still bears an awful social stigma. Some so-called lepers don't even have the disease but the skin lesions of psoriasis, eczema and other conditions can be mistakenly diagnosed as leprosy. One such case is that of Joanna Nightingale in 1468.

Joanna is a wealthy widow of Brentford in Essex. Her family and neighbours believe the unfortunate woman is suffering from leprosy and, if so, she must withdraw from public life of any kind and retire to a leper hospital. All her possessions will be forfeit and, by law, she will be regarded as having died.

DID YOU KNOW?

The last public act of a leper is to attend church for their own funeral.

Joanna isn't going to give up so easily, insisting she doesn't have leprosy and that her family are simply too eager for their inheritance. The relatives persuade the sheriff to summon a jury to decide the widow's fate, but she takes her case to the highest level, paying for expensive lawyers at the Chancery Court. Joanna arranges for King Edward IV's personal physicians to examine her and make a true diagnosis.

William Hattecliffe, Roger Marchall and Dominic de Sergio, the most distinguished medical men in England, make a thorough and detailed examination and find that Joanna shows no sign of leprosy and she is free to return home to Brentwood, her possessions intact. But you have to wonder how her family and neighbours treat her afterwards.

We haven't encountered any female physicians because women couldn't attend university, but nevertheless a few do call themselves so, perhaps having learned their medical skills as John Crophill did, or from fathers, brothers or husbands. One extraordinary malpractice case is worth mentioning because it names a female physician. It happened in the county of Devon in 1350 and was brought against Pernell, 'a woman physician', alongside her husband, Thomas de Rasyn, also a physician. They were accused of causing the death of a miller in Sidmouth because of their ignorance and poor practices. Found guilty, they were made outlaws. Banished from home and with assistance of any kind forbidden from anyone, this was a virtual death sentence. But Pernell and Thomas did not submit: they appealed to King Edward III, receiving a royal pardon and the reinstatement of their reputations. This was an exceptional outcome.[4]

A physician treats Vespasian who is suffering from leprosy (detail).

What is the difference between a physician and a surgeon?

Let us ask a man who knows: Richard Esty, Upper Warden of the Surgeons' Guild of London a number of times between 1459 and 1464. He has written a useful medical handbook:

> Greetings, Master Esty. Can you explain for us why we have physicians and surgeons and why they keep themselves separate?
>
> You can blame his Holiness the Pope for that – not the present incumbent but one of his predecessors – way back in 1215, the year King John sealed the Magna Carta. That year, a papal council was held in the Lateran Palace, wherever that is. The Pope and the cardinals debated many things but there was a worry that churchmen were getting too involved in warfare and passing judgement in criminal cases, resulting in death as the punishment. In their supposedly great wisdom, the council declared no churchman should ever spill a drop of blood. They thought that would deal with both problems – which it didn't – but it created a new and far more serious one.
>
> What was that?
>
> Patience! I'm coming to that. As you know – at least I hope you do – all proper physicians study at university (giving themselves airs and graces because of it, too) and in order to gain a degree they must take minor holy orders. That means all physicians are churchmen of a sort and the papal ruling of 1215 applies to them. Thus, they cannot spill blood. Do you understand so far?
>
> I think so: physicians can't go to war or condemn criminals to death.
>
> What a wooden-head you are. I'm talking about medical practice. It meant physicians could no longer carry out blood-letting, tooth-drawing or perform surgical procedures because that would spill blood. Instead, laymen like myself learned the craft of surgery, doing apprenticeships, instead of book-learning and university. We surgeons are far more practical. We leave the theorising to the physicians and get

on with the task of treating patients' ailments. They may call themselves 'doctors' but we're the masters of our art.

Does that mean nobody could ever be both a physician and a surgeon?

In truth, there is one man, presently in service to the King's Grace, Edward IV, who did his apprenticeship as a surgeon under his father and then went to Cambridge University to study physic and lecture there. Because he had already spilled blood as a surgeon, he couldn't take holy orders but studied all the same. I know not how that was arranged.

Who is this man?

A lecherous fellow, ever likely to bring our noble guild into disrepute. He frequents brothels, despite being a married man. His name is William Hobbys. Avoid him if you can, whatever your medical needs. After all, seems to me, a man can properly ride only one horse at a time, if you take my meaning.

I do, Master Esty. Thank you for speaking to us and for the warning about Hobbys.[5]

I would take Richard Esty's advice, if you can, and would extend it to include medical practitioners in general, unless your case is desperate. Better yet, should you fall sick, come home to the twenty-first century, if at all possible.

Chapter 7

Work and Leisure

What is the attitude to work?

In medieval England everyone is expected to work, if they are able. God has ordained it so. For the king, his nobles and lords, work means administration, government, justice and defence of the realm. Apart from the last, it's pretty much down to paperwork, so secretaries, clerks, scribes, judges and lawyers are involved. Churchmen work at saving souls by praying and preaching, running abbeys, priories, cathedrals and parishes, but more often than not they too are up to their elbows in paperwork. Everything has to be written down, longhand, and often numerous copies have to be made. It's a slow business.

Those who don't fit into these two categories have to do all the other jobs that keep the people fed, clothed, sheltered, clean and healthy, and, if possible, content with their position in society. Of course, few ever are content as everyone hoping to better themselves.

Top tip

Remember, God put you where He wants you to be, so to try and change that is going to upset the Almighty's eternal plan and you won't get much sympathy when you fail.

Only small children, the sick, the 'obviously' disabled and the very elderly are excused from working. By 'obviously' disabled I mean those missing a limb or crippled or totally blind. Being hard of hearing, having a dodgy hip or being on the autistic spectrum isn't going to qualify anyone as being among the 'deserving poor'. The deserving poor get sympathy, handouts of alms and licences to beg. Anyone fit enough to work but unable to find a job is undeserving, regarded as 'idle' and an abomination to society. It's harsh, I know, but that's how it is in medieval times, so you need to find employment of some kind urgently, to pay your way and earn respect.

What kinds of jobs are available?

Fortunately, before the Tudor period unemployment is almost unknown, especially after the plague has severely reduced the population. Unfortunately for you, you haven't had the appropriate training for any of the good jobs, unless you have some sparkling talent that can't fail to impress. In the countryside, agricultural labour will be available year round: ploughing and planting, weeding and bird-scaring, hoeing, reaping and harvesting, carting and threshing, each in its season and all hard, manual work. Perhaps being outdoors in all weathers will suit you, but maybe you had some less muddy employment in mind.

Do you fancy shoe-making, carpentry, book-binding or jewellery-making? If you do, then you'll likely have to live in town, but therein lies the problem. Every town will already have its own craftsmen and they like to keep it that way. Unless you can provide a new service or manufacture something that doesn't exist there – and if it doesn't that's probably because it isn't needed or there aren't enough customers to keep it profitable – then as an outsider you will not be welcome. Worse still, you won't be a member of the guild.

Smaller towns usually have one or two guilds, dedicated to chosen saints, to which the various craftsmen and traders belong. In larger towns and cities each craft may have enough members to form their own exclusive guild, company or fellowship, whatever they decide to call it. Guilds have many functions: overseeing the indenturing (enrolment) and training of apprentices, policing the behaviour of members – and their wives – quality control of the making and selling of goods, insurance for widows, orphans and loss of livelihood, social events, even providing mourners for members' funerals. But one of the guild's most important tasks is to prevent non-members like you from setting up in competition.

Becoming a member is almost impossible. You could choose a craft and pay to be indentured as an apprentice. Your master will give you food and lodging and teach you everything you'll need to know about the craft, the trade secrets, but you won't be paid. It may be seven years or more before you qualify. For example, the goldsmiths of London demand a ten-year term in order to learn the intricacies of their craft, unless your father is a goldsmith, in which case you could qualify sooner because you probably know your way around the tools having watched your father at work. Once you've qualified, you spend a few years working as a 'journeyman' in the craft, being paid a daily wage, but you now have to pay for your keep. You also have to pay your membership fee to the guild if you want to work in the town or city.

While you're a journeyman you'll work on your masterpiece. If you're a goldsmith, it might be a gilded chalice or an exquisite brooch. A stationer dealing with books might make an illuminated manuscript. Whatever it is, your masterpiece has to demonstrate your skills and be made to the highest standard you can manage. When it's finished, the officers of the guild will judge it, and if it passes their discriminating examination, you will be entitled to call yourself a master [or mistress] of the craft, set up your own business and take on and train apprentices. Even then, if you move to another town the guild there may not recognise your qualification.

Another way to become a member is to buy your way in. Money has a knack of opening doors and overriding regulations. If you can't afford the sizeable donation demanded, if you're a woman, there is another way: marry a man who is already a member and learn the craft from him as you go along.

What kinds of jobs are available to women?

Employers like to take on women because, though there are equal opportunities for girls in most trades or crafts – though not in the professions – equal pay for women is out of the question. Female labour is always cheaper. Women cannot be priests, lawyers or, officially, at least, physicians, but they can do just about anything else. Some of the heaviest work, like that of bell-founders and blacksmiths, employs a few women. In the fifteenth century two London widows took over their husbands' bell-casting businesses. Johanna Hill ran the foundry in St Botolph's parish, Aldgate, when her husband, Richard, died in 1440, and did so until her death a year later when John Sturdy seems to have bought the business. John ran the bell foundry until he died, probably in 1459, when his widow – also Johanna – continued to manage the business.

DID YOU KNOW?

In the twenty-first century at least sixteen bells in churches across southern England, from Norfolk to Devon, still bear the makers' marks, showing they were made in the Hill-Sturdy foundry in London.[1]

We also know of a couple of women blacksmiths. A London woman bequeathed 'all my tools and anvil of blacksmithy to my apprentice' in her will. During the Hundred Years' War against the French, there came an occasion when Katherine of Bury, wife to Walter and mother of Andrew – both employed as the king's smiths at the Tower of London – was paid 8d a day 'to keep up the king's forge in the Tower and carry on the work of the forge' following Walter's death while Andrew was away with the king on military campaign. One of Katherine's jobs was to repair and sharpen the tools of the stonemasons working on the royal Palace of Westminster at the time.

A woman blacksmith.

After her father, William Ramsey, died of the plague in 1349, his daughter, Agnes, continued to run his business as an architect and stonemason. Although Agnes was married to Robert Hubard, she kept her father's surname because he was quite famous with an excellent reputation. Agnes continued to work with celebrities of the day, being commissioned to build an exquisite tomb for King Edward III's mother, the dowager Queen Isabella, at the incredible price of £100.

Women working in less remarkable trades are difficult to identify, but because people sometimes took their surnames from their occupations and there are feminine forms of those surnames, you can sometimes discover what jobs women do. Here is a list of names:

Throwster – female silk weaver

Webster – female textile weaver

Huckster – female hawker of food & drink

Brewster – female brewer

Tapster – female ale-seller

Spinster – female spinner of flax or wool

Baxter – female baker

Kempster – carder & comber of wool

Tranter – female street trader

Thaxter – female thatcher

Pallister – female paling-fence maker

Hewster – female hewer of wood

Beggister – female beggar

Whister – female linen-bleacher

Lister or Dyster – female dyer

Corvester – cordwainer [shoemaker]

Barbaress – female barber

Billingster – female agricultural worker

Hucksters and tapsters are so numerous that the female name is generally applied to men doing the same job. In tax returns of the thirteenth century, women are also described as bellringsters, hoardsters, washsters and fillisters. What are 'fillisters'? The OED describes a fillister as a tool used in carpentry; the Free Dictionary website says it's 'a hook and loop fastener'. Perhaps while you're travelling back in history, you can discover what a fillister actually does. [2]

Femmes soles

This term, borrowed from the French, describes a category of women, particularly in larger towns, that have their greatest prominence from the fourteenth century to the late fifteenth. Most women are *'femmes couvertes'*, that is, in the eyes of the law, they are 'covered' by their husbands. This means that although they may work as, say, baxters, while their husbands have quite different occupations, if the women take on apprentices, owe or are owed money, or are found to be selling underweight loaves, the law deals with their husbands. The husbands hold the contracts of apprenticeship, any profits from the women's trade goes to their spouses and it's the husbands who are prosecuted for faulty bread sold and pursued for any debts their wives owe.

However, *'femmes soles'* are women who stand 'alone', not covered by their husbands. Obviously, any widows who continue to run their deceased husbands' businesses come into this category, but married women can also be *femmes soles* – with their husbands' consent in the first place – responsible for their own business contracts, profits and debts. One woman who has made a great success of running her own business as well as taking on her husband's after his death is Rose de Burford. Let's ask her about being a *femme sole*:

Good day, Mistress Burford. Can you tell us about yourself?
I was born in London in King Edward I's reign. My father was Thomas Romayn, Alderman and one-time Lord Mayor of London in 1309-10. He was a wealthy wool merchant and pepperer, importing spices, supplying King Edward II with exotic wares: cloves, cinnamon and sugar among them. I also had contracts with King Edward and Queen Isabella for exquisitely embroidered vestments and trimmings.

So, you're an embroiderer?
No. I don't do the stitching myself. I wouldn't have patience for the couching of silken and gold threads. I employ out-workers and then supervise and coordinate the work. The king commissioned a cope that took a year to make and cost £100.

What's a cope?

You don't know? It's a semi-circular cloak worn by bishops and the like. This one was rich indeed, spangled with coral beads – the finest in Christendom, I think – the queen sent it as a gift to the Holy Father in Rome. Imagine that: it's being worn by the Pope himself! I'm most proud of that.

Did your husband approve of your business?

Of course. It brought in money; why would he not? John de Burford was my father's business partner as a pepperer and wool merchant but was a mercer too. Seeing you're so ignorant: mercers import the finest textiles. When I married John, I learned everything about his various trades too. He was an Alderman and a Sheriff of the City in 1303-04. We hoped he would be elected Lord Mayor in 1322 but he died before that happened, so Hamo de Chigwell, a fishmonger, was elected – again. Since then, there's been a muddle over who's the mayor, betwixt Hamo and the goldsmith, Nicholas de Farndon. It was Lord Mayor Farndon who sent a letter last September, addressed to the Mayor of Dover, demanding to know why Dover had confiscated a shipload of pepper, zedoary and nutmegs of mine, requiring payment of £9 for its release. This was despite a writ from the king, pardoning me of any customs duties *in lieu* of the considerable debt the Royal Wardrobe still owes me.

Was the dispute resolved?

It was and to my satisfaction, except for a barrel-load of zedoary that went missing whilst in their hands.

What's zedoary, you ask? It's a bitter spice from far off India – very expensive.

Thank you, mistress. I won't waste anymore of your valuable time.

Just as well, I have a consignment of sugar to send to the king. Business can't be interrupted for the likes of you. Get you gone.[3]

Rose de Burford was a very wealthy widow owning numerous properties, including tenements in London and country estates in Surrey,

Kent and Sussex. Her own country residence was at Charlton in Kent, but I cannot discover whether that is now Charlton in south London (then in the county of Kent) or a place of the same name near Dover. Either would have been convenient at each end of her business: for sales to customers in the city, or for overseeing the importing of the goods. She could afford to pay for the construction of a chapel on the south side of the church of St Thomas the Apostle in Cullum Street, in Vintry Ward, in the City of London. Rose had a son, James, who became a knight, and a daughter Katherine, for whom I have found no further information.

However wealthy they are and successful in running their businesses, it is a rare thing for women to hold an official appointment. But one woman did so: Alice Holford. Her husband, Nicholas, held the important position of Bailiff of London Bridge, responsible for collecting tolls from ships passing through the drawbridge section of the bridge as well as from carts and wagons crossing the bridge itself. To make matters complicated, the tolls to be paid varied according to the goods being transported, who they belonged to and who was carrying them. When Nicholas died in 1433 Alice took over. The arrangement was probably supposed to be temporary until a new male bailiff could be appointed, but Alice was so efficient and trustworthy that she remained in this very responsible post, collecting the city's customs revenues for twenty years.[4] Not bad for a 'mere' woman, the London authorities must have agreed. Sadly, Alice's success didn't lead to any other women receiving important civic posts.

What do women do if they have no job?

Sadly, if a woman has no skills to offer an employer and cannot find some kind of work as a domestic servant, her options are limited. Weeding other people's gardens is a possibility, but that requires a good knowledge of plants, to be able to tell the desirable ones from the invaders. Washerwomen are always needed, but that job also needs the know-how of soap-making, soaking, beating, stain-removal, linen-whitening, water-recycling, folding, drying, etc. Doing the laundry is hard work and a long process. As a twenty-first century traveller, ignorant of the intricacies of such mundane jobs, there may be one avenue left open to you. As a last resort to earn a living, you can always sell your body. Prostitution is said to be the oldest profession.

DID YOU KNOW?

If you're wondering, the second oldest is spying – both are mentioned in the Bible.

Throughout history, prostitution is seen as a necessary fact of life, for the most part tolerated by civic authorities, if rarely approved. In medieval London the city tries to regulate the work of 'common women', confining them to Cock Lane, in the north-west, near Newgate. But better yet is to keep them outside the city, out of sight and, hopefully, out of mind, across the Thames in Southwark, where they won't sully the city's precious reputation. The Liberty of the Clink is an area in Southwark that comes under the authority of the Bishop of Winchester. Because the liberty lies outside the jurisdiction of the City of London, some activities forbidden there are permitted here.

In 1161 the bishop was granted the power to license prostitutes and brothels in the liberty and the women became known as Winchester Geese. To be 'bitten by a Winchester goose' means to contract a venereal disease and 'goose bumps' is slang for the symptoms. Clients come by boat from a jetty at Stew Lane in the city across the river to avoid being questioned if they pass through the gates at London Bridge, and of course the gates are closed after dusk. As clients approach Bankside, as it's known, there are signs with the brothels' names painted on the white walls: the Bear's Head, the Cross Keys, the Bell and the Swan. Under the direction of the Bishop of Winchester there are some restrictions: the brothels aren't permitted to open on Sundays or religious days. There is some attempt to stop things getting out of hand, with a fine of twenty shillings should any 'woman of the bordello [...] draw any man by his gown or by his hood or any other thing'.

John of Gaddesden, an English physician writing in the early fourteenth century, advised women how to protect themselves against venereal disease. Immediately after sex with any suspect man, he said, the woman should jump up and down, run backwards down the stairs and inhale some pepper to make herself sneeze. Next, she should tickle her vagina with a feather dipped in vinegar to flush infected sperm out of her body, then wash her genitals thoroughly in a concoction of roses and herbs boiled in vinegar. It's hard to imagine anyone actually following this advice, let alone one of the girls in Southwark's stews (brothels). It would have puzzled the customer she'd just serviced for one thing, and running backwards downstairs sounds an excellent way to break your neck. At least it was understood that diseases such as gonorrhoea were spread by sexual intercourse: a big step forward.

In 1321 King Edward II had founded the Lock Hospital in Southwark as a treatment centre for 'lepers', the name then used for anyone with sores and skin lesions. It was located less than a mile from the stews of Bankside and, unsurprisingly, it soon started to specialise in VD cases. 'Lock Hospital' can still be found in slang dictionaries today as a generic term for any VD clinic. Southwark's lucrative trade gave it such place names as Codpiece Lane, Cuckold Court and Sluts' Hole.

Of course, prostitution is by no means confined to London. Every city, town and village probably has an accommodating woman or two and York is no exception. In 1424 in York, Elizabeth Frowe and Joan Skryvener were presented as procuresses, specialising in supplying young women for the entertainment of friars and priests. The borough records of York, dated 12 May 1483, note that 'the whole parish of St Martin in Micklegate came before my lord the mayor and complained of Margery Gray, otherwise called Cherrylips, that she was a woman ill disposed of her body to whom ill disposed men resort to the annoyance of her neighbours'.

What entertainment is available?

Fortunately, life isn't all work in medieval England. The Church has numerous 'holy days', celebrating important Christian events such as Christmas, Shrove Tuesday (Mardi Gras), Easter, Whitsun and Ascension, as well as Church 'inventions', like Lady Day, Corpus Christi and Harvest Festival. Then there are the numerous saints' days. Many of these celebrations, though not all, mean a holiday from work, far more than we have in the twenty-first century and Christmas alone is a twelve-day holiday. There are also a few pagan festivals, remnants of other religions from previous centuries: Hocktide, May Day and Lammas.

Holidays are an excuse for feasting, fun and celebration; along with the appropriate church service in most cases. Shrove Tuesday, on the eve of the forty-day season of Lent, is often celebrated with a football match. Forget City versus United, ninety minutes, eleven-a-side with a referee to see the rules are kept on a nice, neat playing field. This is a free-for-all through the streets; one village against another; fishmongers' apprentices against the grocers' apprentices; wives against unmarried girls (yes, women play as well). Anything goes: kicking (not only the ball), carrying, heading (other players as well as the ball), punching, tripping, hair-pulling and hiding the ball under your skirts.

The aim is to get the ball (an inflated pig's bladder) in the 'goal'; usually the parish church porch at either end of the 'pitch', which maybe a couple of miles apart. Games can have any number of players and go on all day, or until the participants drop from exhaustion and are required to be revived in the nearest tavern, and a great time is had by all. Tomorrow will be a day of sore heads, whether from butting the ball or each other, or drinking too much ale in celebrating victory or consolation in defeat. Casualties are many, with even the occasional fatality. Football is a hazardous sport.

For something less energetic, there is likely to be street theatre of some kind. Acrobats, minstrels, jugglers and mountebanks, even puppet shows delight spectators. Mystery, miracle and mummers' plays are staged.

The popular medieval mystery plays re-enacted Bible stories and first appear in the tenth and eleventh centuries, acted out by monks, priests and choristers as a way of helping ordinary folk learn the biblical stories. However, the Church is soon worrying about churchmen performing certain parts in these plays. Should a monk play Eve or the Virgin Mary, or worse still, King Herod murdering the innocent babies? Is it appropriate to tell of a woman giving birth or mass murder in a church? Soon lay members are acting the parts – men only, so historians tells us – and the scripts become longer, the stories more involved, taking on a traditional form so a town has the exact same plays, year after year, with the scripts passed on by word of mouth only.

Gradually, more and more mystery plays are created and eventually the whole Bible story is told, from the Creation to Doomsday, including Adam and Eve, Cain and Abel, Noah's Flood, the Nativity, Crucifixion and

Street performers.

Resurrection, gathered together in cycles. The entire cycle is performed in one day, usually close to Christmas or Easter, though in York they choose the feast of Corpus Christi in June, which gives them more hours of daylight as the cycle takes place outdoors around the city.

The plays were originally performed in the churchyard and crowds would gather to watch, but, as you can imagine, the actors could get carried away and the plays became more and more rude. The clergy complained about the lewdness debasing the scriptural message, so the cycles are moved out of the churchyard and onto the streets, where they become worse still.

There are no stages so the actors devise two-tier pageant wagons that can be wheeled around to the required venue, the two levels providing performance space with the ground in front of the wagon forming a third stage. Each Bible story has its own scenery which is fixed to the wagon. In cities like Chester and York, each guild has their own pageant wagon and tells one particular story – the goldsmiths of York always do the Three Kings with their expensive gifts and jewellery, the water-drawers of Chester always enact Noah's flood, though the ship-wrights do the building of the ark. The wagons trundle round town in the correct order, performing the story and then moving on.

When the dramas are performed by secular folk, professional actors are sometimes hired to play the roles; deductions being made from their pay for poor acting or forgetting their lines. These actors are considered the lowest of the low, along with beggars and vagabonds, and the Church frowns upon their involvement in religious plays. However, even the amateur actors throw themselves into their parts. When Father Nicholas de Neuchatel played Christ in the Easter Passion of 1437, he almost died on the cross and had to be attended by a physician and the local tavern landlady. It's not recorded whose attentions had the greater effect upon his recovery.

Usually, there is little money, unless the guilds provide funds by taxing their members, so players perform in their everyday clothes, though characters such as God have special robes and a mask. There is a record of an actor paying a goldsmith's wife for the loan of her best dress so he could play the part of Noah's wife: the original pantomime dame.

DID YOU KNOW?

Noah's wife is the original pantomime dame. On the Continent, hers is a very minor role, but in England she has a unique comedy role as the stereotypical cantankerous and obstinate wife, adding to the fun.

However the props and costumes are cobbled together, the plays provide a wonderful entertainment in the towns and cities, bringing colour and a sense of drama. The other kind of religious drama is the Miracle Plays which tell the stories of the saints and, obviously, their miracles. The earliest that survives is about St Catherine and was specially written by Abbot Geoffrey of St Albans in 1110 for his pupils.

For poorer villages and hamlets there is another form of spectacle; less expensive and of shorter duration. This less ambition form of play has its own class of actors, the mummers, and is quite different from the Mystery Plays of the cities. Mumming is an ancient form of street theatre dating back long before Christianity as a fertility rite, marking the death of summer and its rebirth in the spring. The word 'mumming' refers to the masks the actors wear to disguise themselves during the performance. This disguise is important because it's thought that if a mummer is recognised, the magic of the ritual is ruined and the sun might not return. The tradition continues that mummers should be unrecognisable. Morris men are part of this same custom with their ribbons, bells and blacked-up faces, making them hard to recognise. It's because of their blackened faces that they are called 'Morris' or more correctly 'Moorish', i.e., African men.

By the Middle Ages mumming has lost its pagan significance. People are no longer so worried that the sun might not return, though enough of the old practices are kept up, just in case. The mummers are now actors and their performances purely for entertainment and money. A hat is usually passed around the crowd to collect donations, not for charity but for the actors to earn a living. Medieval Christianity introduced new characters to the mummers' plays. Beelzebub is now a popular baddie, but the most important new character was the hero, St George, who became famous after supposedly slaying a dragon in Egypt in the third century AD. St George is sometimes accompanied by his dragon, which symbolises evil of any kind, but since the dragon costume is difficult and expensive to make his place is often taken by other, less outlandish, villains. After the Crusades, this is often the Saracen or Turkish knight but can be any manner of wicked king, demon or thief; there were endless possibilities. Mummers' plays always have a moral, that good will always, after many a set-back, conquer evil.

How would I relax?

By the fifteenth century, as more people become literate, a new way of relaxing evolves: reading for pleasure. In England in 1481 William Caxton, using the first printing press in the country, publishes *The History of Reynard the Fox*. Caxton intends to educate his readers, using the short stories of Reynard to show them how to avoid the 'daily deceptions' of life. But this is far from a serious book. If you've ever watched and enjoyed the cartoon antics of the Roadrunner and Wily Coyote, or Tom and Jerry, you will love Reynard the Fox.

If you prefer romance and adventure novels with a dash of fantasy thrown in, Master Caxton has another printed gem for you: *Le Morte d'Arthur* by Sir Thomas Malory. Despite its French title, don't worry, Sir Thomas wrote his best-seller in English – well, Middle English, at least: a language you'll be getting used to by now. The book is a collection of tales about King Arthur and the Knights of the Round Table. You'll hear about familiar characters such as Arthur, Guinevere, Merlin and Sir Lancelot, as well as some that may be new to you: Tristram and Isolde, Elaine, Sir Bedevere and Sir Gawain.

For something a tad more racy, there is *The Romance of the Rose*, marketed as 'a handbook for lovers' when it was first written, in French, in the thirteenth century. After Geoffrey Chaucer translates it into English in the fourteenth century, this bawdy 'dream-tale' becomes very popular. There are some exquisitely illuminated versions of *The Rose* still extant in the twenty-first century and, if you're lucky, you may find other manuscript copies during your travels. The pictures are gorgeous to look at, even if you don't fancy wading through the very wordy text.

Chapter 8

Family Matters

And, son, if you want to have a wife,
Do not choose her for her wealth,
But look, son, she will be your life;
You must consider wisely and take advise,
That she be good, honest and wise.
Though she be poor, take no notice of that
For she shall do you better service
Than shall a rich woman, without doubt.[1]

These lines are taken from a long poem *How The Wise Man Taught His Son,* a set of fifteenth-century instructions for the youth of the time about the best ways to get on in life. The son is advised to marry a poor woman as she'll make a better wife than a rich one. The poem goes on to say that it's better to have just a dish of pottage and peace and quiet, than a huge feast but an angry and heavy heart. Despite this advice, as we'll see, marrying for money was the hope of many bachelors.

Marriage

In medieval England marriage doesn't require a church service. In 1399 John Esyngwald and Elizabeth Snawe were brought before the Church Court in York Minster, accused of having sex without being married. They appeared before the Dean, claiming that they were indeed married. Apparently, John had said, in private, 'I take you, Elizabeth, to my wife and to this I plight you my troth'. In return, Elizabeth had said, 'I take you to my husband and to this I plight you my troth'. Although John went on to swear on the holy gospels that the contract would be made public as soon as convenient, the Church accepted that the couple were already man and wife and their acts of fornication were within marriage and, therefore, legal.[2]

A simple exchange of vows between a couple – made in the tavern, the street or even in bed – followed by 'consummation' (i.e., sex), is considered a valid marriage by the Church. No witnesses are required so it can be difficult for either party to prove or disprove they are married afterwards. It can be a worry as to whether or not a couple are legally wed, especially if the woman discovers she is with child. There is always the possibility that the man may deny having ever made any vow, if his only purpose was to enjoy himself on a Saturday night behind the ale-house.

John Borell, a wax-chandler in London, while still an apprentice, had an affair with Maud Clerk, a maid servant in the household of a disreputable priest, Father Jeffrey. Once John qualified and set up his own shop he wanted to marry a respectable young woman, Letitia. Everything was arranged for their wedding in St Paul's Cathedral, but as the ceremony reached the point where it was asked if there was any impediment or objection to the marriage, Father Jeffrey stood up, claiming John was already wed to his serving girl, Maud. John denied it but the priest and Maud demanded compensation. The dispute went to court and poor Letitia – the innocent bride – saw all her dowry wasted on lawyers and fines to be paid by her new husband. Their marriage was confirmed as valid but the newly-weds were almost penniless.[3]

If you are considering marrying some suitable spouse back in time, at least you won't have to worry about being too closely related for your union to be legal. Nobody has ever considered a great great ... etc. grandparent marrying their great great ... etc. grandchild, so you'll be fine on that account. However, others have to consider a number of other relationships that the Church has deemed to not be permitted. These regulations were all set out by the Pope at the Lateran Council meeting in 1215 (the one at which it was decided churchmen must not spill blood, see Chapter 6). The rules apply to everyone, but if you can afford it, you can buy a 'dispensation' from the Pope so the Church will overlook the fact that you plan to marry your second cousin once removed, or whatever. This is often necessary for kings, princes and nobles because European royals are so interrelated. This doesn't make for healthy breeding stock so the rules do make sense, even if the rich often break them. There are other relations, though, that are forbidden to marry and which don't seem to make sense. The future King Richard III, when he was just the Duke of Gloucester, married his second cousin once removed, Anne Neville. Let's ask the king to explain about the dispensations required:

> Your Grace, I beg you to forgive the intrusion but I hear you required a number of dispensations from the Pope in order to marry your wife, Anne.
>
> I don't know what business it is of yours but I have a few moments before I open Parliament so ... it happened thus. Back in 1471, my brother, King Edward IV, God assoil him, wanted me to wed the Lady Anne Neville, younger daughter of the Earl of Warwick. Warwick and I were first cousins, making Anne my second cousin once removed, so a dispensation was necessary to overcome that impediment to our union. Moreover, Anne was recently widowed, having been wed previously to Prince Edward of Lancaster, a more distant cousin to me, the Devil take the wretch. To wed a cousin's widow likewise requires a dispensation.
>
> That must have cost a deal of money, sire?
>
> Of course it did. His Holiness demands payment at every turn. It was as well that Edward was dealing with all the legal details and sending the money to Rome. At the time, I couldn't have afforded it. And more was yet required for my elder brother, George, Duke of Clarence, was already wed to Anne's elder sister, Isabel Neville. That made Anne and me sister- and brother-in-law twice over, for which impediment another double dispensation was needed.
>
> This must have been getting very expensive, sire.
>
> You jest? And we have yet another chapter in this saga. My lady-mother, the Duchess of York, is Anne's godmother. That makes Anne my sister in the eyes of God, requiring another dispensation be purchased.
>
> At least, after all those documents were gathered together, there can be no doubt that your marriage to the queen is legal in every way.

Well, I hope so. You see, we didn't await the arrival of so much paperwork. King Edward was eager to have us wed. We married on trust that the Pope would grant all the dispensations required, despite my brother George trying to bribe the Holy Father not to do so. He wanted all Warwick's inheritance for himself, through Isabel, you understand. King Edward dealt with everything, filed away all the documents. In truth, I'm not sure we received everything required but you are sworn to secrecy on that score. Break your oath to me and you'll not relish the consequences.

Never, sire. You can trust me. Cross my heart: I'll never tell a soul. Thank you for taking the trouble to explain. Thank you, Your Grace.

Oh, do cease your grovelling and be on your way. I have a realm to govern.[4]

A marriage ceremony.

Divorce

Before you think about marriage, you had best be certain you have the right partner because divorce isn't an option for anyone but royalty, unless one partner can't manage the conjugal rights, in which case your union can be annulled because it hasn't been consummated. If you're a woman, however, you'll have to prove it. If a husband takes his wife to a Church Court and swears that she either can't or won't oblige him in the marriage bed, his case will be taken seriously and she'll be forced to do as she's told: there's no such thing as rape within marriage. But if a woman takes her husband to court for the same reason, matters get more complicated.

For example, in July 1432 in York, John Skathelok was put to the test. A group of prostitutes, arranged by the Church Court, went to John, undressed him, touched him and let him touch them in return: all to no effect. His wife, Alice, was examined by midwives who reported that she was 'well formed', strong and willing, but John had never 'known her carnally' since their marriage, nor any other woman, as the prostitutes had shown. All the facts were reported back to the court, in detail.[5] Poor John: these were grounds enough for the marriage to be annulled as though it had never taken place and his reputation with the ladies probably never recovered. Alice was free to find a new husband who could do his duty in the bedchamber.

Within marriage it is expected that the woman must be faithful, but not necessarily the husband. This is because any child she bears is assumed to be his and no man is likely to want to be responsible for some other fellow's offspring. If the husband is unfaithful, there are no such consequences – unless for the other woman's partner – so courts rarely hear cases brought by wives whose spouses have strayed, though it does happen.

Alice Hobbys had been wed to William for twenty years and they had five children. At Christmas time 1475, when some gossipy neighbours told Alice her husband had been seen in a brothel, Alice confronted him. William admitted he'd been committing adultery with any number of prostitutes in London, Southwark and northern France since 1462. Alice was so disgusted she 'rejected his embraces and refused to fulfill the marital debt', i.e., wouldn't have sex with him anymore. This last was his major complaint when Alice sued him for divorce in the Church Court. They were, seemingly, a respectable couple but the proceedings revealed William in a new light. He was a surgeon, serving King Edward IV – his time in France had been in the king's service – and a prominent member of the Barber-Surgeons' Guild of London. During the enquiry a number of William's fellow surgeons, including the Master of the Guild and Hobbys' own son-in-law, came forward to tell of the occasions when they'd seen William visiting brothels.

Two surgeons told of one evening when they had been summoned to treat a Southwark brothel-keeper, wounded by a disgruntled customer. Happening to glance through a hole in the wall into another room, the pair were shocked to see William in bed with a young prostitute. Such outrageous behaviour brought a stern warning from the Master of the Guild, who happened to be one of the eye-witnessses.[6]

In response to the testimony of numerous reputable men, the court found in Alice's favour, granting her a divorce from William, but this wasn't the complete break we would expect in the twenty-first century. She was no longer required to share William's house or his bed, nor to eat at his table, but they were still considered to be married in the eyes of the law and neither party could wed anyone else until they became widowed. Alice outlived William but never remarried.

How are women treated?

On the whole, women aren't treated too badly in medieval England. Although arranged marriages are a fact of life, especially among the wealthy and titled, true love matches do happen. This case among the Norfolk gentry folk, in 1469, shows how difficult love can make life. Margery, the eldest daughter of Margaret Paston, did the unthinkable and fell in love with the family's steward, Richard Calle, and they married in secret. When the family found out, they were horrified and tried to keep the couple apart. Here is part of a love letter Richard wrote to Margery:

> My own lady and mistress and very true wife [...] It seems a thousand years ago since I spoke with you and I had rather be with you than possess all the goods in the world. Alas, alas, good lady, those that keep us asunder remember full little what they do [...]

I sent you a letter from London by my lad, and he told me he could not speak with you, as a careful watch was kept upon both him and you [...] I suppose that they think we are not contracted together [married] ...[despite] how plainly I spoke to my mistress [Margery's mother, Margaret Paston] at the beginning [...]

I marvel much that they should take this matter so hard [...] considering it is such a case as cannot be remedied [...] and there should be no obstacle against it [...] I pray you let no creature see this letter. As soon as you have read it, let it be burned.[7]

Clearly, Margery couldn't bear to burn her lover's letter, else we would not know of it. The Pastons utterly disapproved. In a letter written by Margery's brother, John, to their eldest brother, he calls Margery 'ungracious' and stresses the fact that Richard Calle's family are only merchants. John is a snob: the Pastons themselves are only a couple of generations on from yeoman farmers.

Margaret Paston, matriarch of the family, had the couple summoned to appear before the Bishop of Norwich. They were questioned separately and the bishop reminded Margery of the shame her marriage brought upon her family, asking if she's certain her secret vow to Richard is sufficiently binding that their union isn't in doubt. Margery says if the words of her vow are not enough, she will make them more certain, for she is bound to Richard in God's eyes, whatever the words are. Richard's story confirmed Margery's. The bishop didn't want to upset the influential Pastons and postponed his decision until later. In the meantime, he sent Margery home.

However, her mother, Margaret, had already decided and sent a message to Margery, saying she would never again be welcome under her roof. Margery returned to Norwich to beg the bishop's help. He found lodgings for her and eventually decided that their marriage was valid. Margery's elder brother, Sir John, demanded that it be annulled, but having calmed down, wanted a proper, official wedding to be conducted quickly. Margaret was less forgiving, saying, 'We have lost of her but a worthless person, and [...] if he [Calle] were dead at this hour, she should never be at my heart as she was.'[8]

Top tip

Marriage can be so casual an affair as to be almost accidental. As for true love... well that too may prove fraught with problems. Choose carefully.

How are children treated?

In the twenty-first century, when we talk about 'swaddling' a baby, we mean wrapping it securely in a blanket to keep it warm and comfortable while it sleeps and statistics show that restless infants sleep longer when swaddled in this way. However, in medieval times, swaddling is an art form, learned by girls practising on their younger siblings and involving numerous layers and great lengths of swaddling 'bands'. The intension is to make certain the child's limbs grow straight and to immobilise the little one and keep him out of harm's way. In case this task falls to you during your travels, here's how to swaddle a baby.

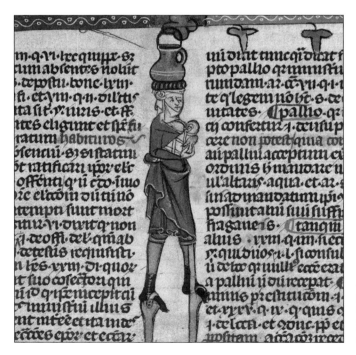

A woman multi-tasking, fetching water whilst breastfeeding her swaddled baby.

First, the baby wears a linen shirt; a simple 'T'-shaped garment open down the front. Most important is the tailclout: a double layer of linen to go around the baby's bottom. Tailclouts are often reinforced with a flannel square or 'pilch', especially overnight, but leakage is a problem. Next, the 'bed': a wide cloth that goes from the baby's chest, down over its feet and up the back. A bib is laid under the chin to catch dribbles or, if the little one is teething and dribbling a lot, a more substantial 'pinafore' might be pinned there instead.

It's vital to keep the baby's head warm, beginning with a 'cross-cloth', a linen band across his forehead. Then a close-fitting woollen cap called a 'biggin', sometimes with a second, looser cap or a hood worn as well. For very young babies needing head support, wide linen 'stay bands' go over the head and are pinned to the shoulders of the shirt.

Top tip

All these pins are dressmaker's pins, not safety pins, so mind you use them with care so they don't stick into the poor baby.

With the baby's head fixed in position, the rest of his body is swaddled with linen strips about three inches wide, or woollen in cold weather. These are wrapped around, beginning at the chest, working down to the feet and back up again, making certain there are no creases to cause discomfort. In tiny babies, the arms are held at its sides by the swaddling but as the baby grows older, the arms are left free. If this sounds like a lot of effort, don't forget the infant will have to be unwrapped and rewrapped every time its tailclout needs changing.

But infants aren't swaddled continuously. They're allowed to crawl around and the swaddling can come off altogether when the child can sit up. Busy mothers sometimes 'lace' unswaddled youngsters into the cradle, making a sort of net across it to keep them from falling out, leaving them free to kick or move about within the cradle. Sometimes, babies are swaddled onto boards to be carried around and these boards have a loop of rope fixed to the back so the little one can be hung up on a hook to watch what's going on without getting in the way, or even hung safely in a tree while mother works in the fields.

Coroners' Court rolls show that whatever precautions are taken, children have accidents. Swaddled infants or those laced into a cradle are known to die in fires. Parents are warned not to sleep with their babies for fear of overlaying and smothering them. Once a child is moving around, the dangers increase. Adventurous toddlers fall down wells, into ponds and streams, tumble into fires and boiling cauldrons, or even crawl out into the street to be crushed by a passing cart. Unexpected accidents happen: there's no such thing as a baby-proof household, but court records show it's rare to leave infants or toddlers unattended.

Babies who aren't swaddled are often simply naked or wrapped in blankets against the cold. There is an image of Jesus as a toddler wearing just his open-fronted shirt and nothing else, which must have made toilet-training easier. A baby's mother is usually its primary carer in poorer families and breastfeeding is free and vital. Poorer parents rarely hire a wet nurse unless the mother dies or is too ill to feed the baby. If no wet nurse is available, other means of feeding include soaking bread or a rag in milk for the child to suckle, or pouring milk into his mouth from a horn. These methods are difficult and the baby's chances of contracting illness increase due to poor hygiene and the lack of beneficial breast milk to help him fight disease. However, among wealthier folk, wet nurses are common and frequently stay on once the infant is weaned, to care for him through childhood. Even so, mothers are encouraged by the Church to nurse their children themselves.

All children are consoled when they fall over or become sick. They're bathed and sung to sleep, even having their meat chewed for them. The average medieval child is loved, even if his fragile life might not last a year.

How are children educated?

Thomas Tusser was a Tudor commentator who generally gave housewives good and sensible advice, and his instructions apply equally to medieval education [I've modernised the spelling]:

> We find it not spoken so often for nought,
> That children were better unborn than untaught,
> Some cockneys with cocking are made very fools,

Fit neither for prentice, for plough, nor for schools.
Teach child to ask blessing, serve God, and to church,
Then bless as a mother, else bless him with birch.
Thou housewife thus doing, what further shall need?
But all men to call thee good mother indeed.

This passage covers all that's required to educate a young child: a task undertaken most usually by its mother or, perhaps, by its nurse, if the mother isn't around. The word 'Cockney' originally meant a boy-child, spoilt and coddled and therefore effeminate. 'Cocking Mams' are over-indulgent mothers whose children are unsuited to being apprenticed, working the land, or even going to school in the future. So Rule No.1 is 'Do not indulge the child.'

The first thing a child learns is the Lord's Prayer or *Paternoster*, the Creed or *Credo* and the Hail Mary or *Ave Maria*. The Creed is the litany recited at mass, beginning 'I believe in one God'. At a baby's baptism, the godparents promise not only to keep their godchild safe 'from the perils of fire and water', but to teach him the basics of the Christian faith. These words, originally in Latin and often together with a basic ABC and numbers, are written on horn books.

DID YOU KNOW?

Horn books aren't really books but a sheet of parchment (later paper), covered with a transparent layer of horn to protect it, put in a wooden frame, shaped like a small, square table-tennis bat, complete with a handle, so the child can hold it easily. These hard-wearing teaching aids often pass down the generations.

A few words about godparents: in medieval times, child-birth is a women-only affair. The mother may be in labour for days and needs every encouragement from her female relatives, friends and neighbours. These women also have to be on hand to stand as godparents at short notice, if the baby seems unlikely to live and requires immediate baptism. Godparents are also known as 'godsibs' or siblings in God. As you can imagine, a group of women sitting around for days do a lot of chatting, and as they run out of topics to discuss probably resort to exchanging rumours. This activity is known as 'godsibing' or gossiping.

Children as young as three are expected to attend church and understand when to bow their heads or kneel in prayer, and to reverence God. They also join in family prayers with the household. Thus, Rule No.2 is 'Teach the child to respect God and the Church'.

You may hate Thomas Tusser's final instruction: the use of corporal punishment. Beating children is now unlawful in most modern societies but medieval folk have other ideas. 'Bless him with birch', as Tusser says. In other words, a good thrashing never does anyone any harm. Physical discipline is thought vital to achieving both learning and manners and children are expected to take it with good grace, even welcoming it as one aspect of the best educational methods. It teaches them to respect authority. If a child misbehaves, there's no point trying to reason with him because children don't know good conduct from bad. So Rule No.3 is 'Do not be lenient: a beating does far more good than harm and is vital to a child's education.'

Pets

You'll discover that medieval folk live closely alongside animals. A poor family may share their home with a cow or goat and a few chickens, sharing warmth in winter and safety at night. Horses and oxen plough and pull carts. Dogs guard property and herd sheep. A knight has his destrier and a miller has cats to keep the vermin from the grain. Animals provide food, clothing and carry burdens. However, we have another need, companionship, and pets of many kinds fulfill this need.

Cats and small dogs are the most popular pets, but squirrels, birds, badgers and even monkeys and popinjays [parrots] amuse their owners, providing comfort and demonstrating their status. In Leonardo da Vinci's painting of a *Lady with an Ermine,*[9] a tame stoat with fur to trim the most luxurious garments is obviously included to show the sitter's nobility.

Cats are a conundrum to medieval minds. They're useful as they catch mice and rats, and cats' fur is one of the few skins that lower-class folk can wear for warmth, according to the Sumptuary Laws of 1363, but cats have a devilish side. Edward, Duke of York, wrote a book about hunting, *The Master of the Game,* in the early fifteenth century and noted 'if any beast hath the devil's spirit, it is the cat'. He explained: a cat torments a mouse or bird before eating it, just as the Devil torments sinners before swallowing them down into Hell.

However, cats can redeem their reputations. Exeter Cathedral has cats on the payroll, receiving 1d per week to supplement their diet of rats and mice and a cat-sized hole lets them come through the wall of the north transept in pursuit of vermin. According to a thirteenth-century guide for women who became anchoresses, the *Ancrene Riwle,* cats are the only companions permitted to them in their self-imposed solitary confinement, but they must not give love to the cats that more rightly belongs to God.

The Countess Eleanor, wife of Simon de Montfort, bought a cat for 2d in 1265. However, others thought their cats were more valuable. In 1294 William Yngeleys brought a court case against his neighbours who took his cat, an animal worth at least 6d, according to William.

In an English Bestiary of the early thirteenth century, cats are given the briefest mention, but thanks to the lively imagination of the illuminator of the manuscript, the accompanying miniature is more informative. The illustration shows three cats – two grey and one black – against a dark blue background with a design of moons and stars in gold to indicate the animals' nocturnal activities. One grey cat has caught a large black mouse or a rat in its paws. The black cat is demonstrating its cleverness, trying to open a cage to get at the small bird within. And we are all familiar with the third cat, also grey, curled up asleep, choosing the cosiest place in the house next to the fire. The illuminator knows more about cats than the author of the manuscript.

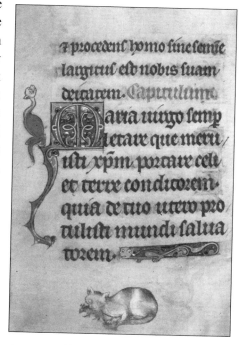

A pet cat with a mouse.

The same author is obviously a dog lover, and in the Bestiary dogs receive six pages of text, describing them as having 'more understanding than any other beast'. They track creatures of the forest using their sense of smell, guard sheep and their masters' property, as well as defending their owners. So far, so good. Unfortunately, so the author says, puppies' tongues are an excellent cure for wounds of the intestines since dogs can heal wounds by licking them. (In a medieval medical text, a remedy for gout consisted solely of boiled puppies too young to have their eyes open.) Our Bestiary author tells a number of classical tales concerning dogs so loyal that they refused to leave their dead or dying masters. However, the historical example shows this wasn't always the case.

DID YOU KNOW?

King Richard II had a pet dog called Math. The animal was with the king when his cousin, Henry Bolingbroke, took him prisoner and demanded he relinquish the crown. When Richard finally gave in to Henry's demands, Math deserted his previous master and went to Henry's side. Assuming the title Henry IV, apparently, the new king took Math's change of loyalty as a good omen for his reign and the loyalty of England to the new regime.

Matters didn't work out quite as well as Henry hoped; dogs are not infallible when it comes to foretelling the future.

Lap dogs are a useful accessory for fine ladies. Not only are they status symbols and companions, in cold, draughty castles, they make the perfect living hot water bottles to warm the ladies' hands or feet. Some noble ladies adore their little lap dogs to the extent that they want them included on their memorials and tombs, to be remembered forever alongside their mistresses. The Arundel tomb in Chichester Cathedral in Sussex shows a dog keeping his lady's feet warm for eternity. At St George's Church in Trotton, also in Sussex, the early fourteenth-century memorial brass of Margaret, Lady Camoys, also has a little dog at her feet, and at Norbury in Derbyshire Margaret Fitzherbert is accompanied in death by her tiny dog. Elsewhere, clerics, dukes and knights are depicted on tombs and brasses with their favourite pooches. But this wasn't just an English tradition: French nobles and their wives, and the Counts of Flanders and their ladies all wanted their pets' company in the hereafter.

Chapter 9

Warfare

Medieval England under the Plantagenet kings is usually at war with someone. Most often, it's the French who are the enemy, but the Scots and Welsh are contenders too during this era in history. The chronicler, Jean Froissart, wrote about The Hundred Years War, a name first coined around 1850 for a series of campaigns that lasted, on and off, from 1337 until 1456. Although Froissart was from the Low Countries, he knew the English well enough to observe: 'The English will never love or honour their King unless he be victorious and a lover of arms and war against their neighbours and especially against such as are greater and richer than themselves'. For the nobility, an added bonus may be had from the spoils of war, such as ransoms, bribes received for leaving places untouched and the looting that sometimes went on. But for the common soldiers these rewards are modest, if they exist at all, and for everyone involved in warfare there is always the chance of injury or death.

How often would I go to war?

This is a tricky question and the answer depends on who you are. If you are a young man, serving in a lord's retinue, you will be trained in the arts of war, and if the opportunity arises, you'll be eager to put your courage and skills to the test. But sometimes those without skills, armed only with the enthusiasm for a fight, find themselves on the battlefield. For example, during the Barons' Wars of the 1260s Simon de Montfort, Earl of Leicester, included the London Trained Bands in his army at the battle of Lewes in Sussex in 1264. Despite their name, they weren't trained for war to any great degree and mainly comprised apprentices and labourers. Unsurprisingly, when facing a charge by the Lord Edward's cavalry, the Londoners turned and fled in the direction of home.

117

Unwittingly though, the Bands still helped Simon to win the day because the Lord Edward – later King Edward I – and his youthful knights were also inexperienced in war and left the battle in pursuit of the fleeing Bands. This left Edward's father, the hapless King Henry III, facing de Montfort. The king lost the day and became de Montfort's pawn in the government of England. Incidentally, Simon actually made a good job of organising Parliament and ruling the country until Edward, having learned his lesson well, turned the tables on his one-time mentor and defeated and killed Simon at the battle of Evesham in 1265.[1] During times of civil war like this, almost anyone could find themselves involved in the fight.

King Henry V knew this, having fought in a civil war battle at Shrewsbury in 1403. He was only Prince of Wales at the time but fought alongside his father, Henry IV, to put down a rebellion raised by Henry Percy, Earl of Northumberland, along with Percy's son, Hotspur, and their Welsh ally, Owain Glyn Dwr.[2] Let's ask King Henry V, an expert on warfare, about his experiences:

> Your Grace, may I ask you about your experiences of civil war and the continuing conflicts in France?
>
> I suppose. If God wills it?
>
> We've never met in person before, sire, but I've seen your portrait. Meeting you now, I see why you were painted in profile. Is that dreadful scar on your cheek a war wound?
>
> You dare ask such a question? Yes, it is. I took an arrow in the face at the battle of Shrewsbury.
>
> Surely, you wore a protective helmet with a face guard?
>
> Of course I did – and we term it a helm and visor. But it was July and hot indeed. A water-carrier offered me a drink and I was in need. A moment's youthful carelessness ... I raised my visor without turning aside from the fray. Some bastard Welsh archer got a lucky shot and I have suffered for it ever since.
>
> But you survived, sire.
>
> Master Bradmore, my surgeon, did as good a job as any man could hope and God guided his hand, of course. The scar still troubles me sometimes but I had to live since I was destined to be king.'

You certainly were, sire, and now that you are, you pursue this war in France. Why is that?

Because the crown of France is also mine by the right of inheritance from Edward III. Every English king worthy of the name makes war on the French.

But isn't that very expensive?

Of course but sometimes it's a greater cost not to.

How come, sire?

You haven't learned your history, have you? Is it not obvious that a decent foreign war keeps the English nobles united and busy fighting a common enemy? Otherwise, being trained for little else besides war, they fight among themselves and civil strife is a more dreadful thing. Fighting the French means peace at home. To keep my visor closed wasn't the only thing I learned at Shrewsbury.

The English had a recent victory against the French at Agincourt. I heard it was a miracle.

The odds were very much against us, the French greatly outnumbering us, but then we had God on our side which made it still an uneven match – but in our favour. God saw to it that we won so, yes, it was a miracle. Only my cousin, the Duke of York, was a noble casualty, drowning in the mud under his fallen horse.

I heard it said that the English longbow won the day. Is that true?

The common archers did well, I admit, but don't discount my noble knights. Now either pick up a weapon and join the ranks or step aside and let us get on with the task of conquering these frog-eating French. I have a crown to win, since God wills it.

The English kings probably don't like to admit that the longbow is their secret weapon because the archers are common folk, but everyone realises how much Edward III and Henry V owe to the skill of the longbowmen. Wanting to be certain that future generations will have the same capability and because it takes years to build up the muscle and bone structure to shoot a bow, archery practice is compulsory, by law. Every able-bodied male between the ages of twelve and sixty

Shooting at the butts during compulsory archery practice.

has to 'shoot at the butts', i.e., straw targets, after church on Sundays. Women are welcome to join in; you never know when a shortage of manpower may call the girls into action.

Top tip

Get your terms right. You never 'fire' an arrow. Arrows are shot or loosed from the bow. Cannon and the new fangled 'gounes' are fired.

What sort of warfare would I practise?

England's ultimate weapon in the fourteenth and early fifteenth century is the longbow. This is a six-foot-long stave of maple or yew with a string of linen, hemp or animal sinew. An experienced longbowman can shoot ten or twelve arrows a minute and their rapid hail against an advancing army is devastating, demoralising and maddening for the horses. The range is almost 300 yards, can be lethal up to about 165 yards and is capable of penetrating chain-mail armour. However, the longbow does have limitations, being mainly a weapon of defence and most effective against advancing enemy cavalry. It's not much use if the enemy fails to advance or if the site of battle is poorly chosen. The longbow is peculiar to the English armies, the French preferring crossbows which have a longer range but are so much slower in shooting:

perhaps three bolts a minute. The most skilled crossbowmen are the Genoese mercenaries, frequently employed by the French.

If you're not an archer (and without having practised since you were twelve, you're unlikely to excel with a bow), there is the chance to join the men-at-arms, including the knights banneret (paid 4s a day), knights bachelor (paid 2s a day) and esquires (1s a day). Men-at-arms on both sides are always mounted, so you'll need to know how to ride, although they dismount to fight if it seems advantageous to do so. They carry a lance of 10-12ft in length, made of wood, but terminating in a metal spearhead or *glaive*. Also a long sword and a short dagger called a *miserichord* or 'mercy' because it can be used to dispatch the mortally wounded. There are other weapons that a mounted man-at-arms might choose, including the battle axe or hammer or a spiked club or mace. For protection, he usually wears a *haulberk*, a coat of mail made by riveting or soldering together small rings of iron or steel; or a *gambeson*, a quilted tunic of boiled leather and stuffed with fleece. Over the top, as additional protection, he may also have added a leather surcoat or *jupon*. The light cavalry, known as *hobelars*, are paid 1s a day and wear light armour such as metal hats, steel gauntlets and 'jacks'; short, quilted coats with iron studs. As head protection, *bascinets* are the fashion in 1346 at the time of the battle of Crécy. The *bascinets* worn by the French nobility have snout-like visors with breathing holes. Even the horses are protected to some extent with armour known as *bards*, not surprisingly since a good warhorse can cost in excess of £100.

The foot soldiers carry a 6-ft pike with a heavy metal head for which designs vary, giving it various names: pike, bill, halberd, etc. They may also carry short swords and bucklers; small shields for hand-to-hand combat. As head protection, unlined metal kettle hats are most convenient and double as water carriers and cooking pots. By the early fourteenth century cannon are also coming onto the battlefield, although their range and accuracy are poor and the contraptions as likely to kill the cannoneer as his opponents. Their main effectiveness is as a means of scaring the enemy, and, in particular, causing his horses to bolt.

It is believed that cannon were used by the English at the battle of Crécy in 1346 as Jean Froissart wrote: 'The English had with them two of the bombards and they made two or three discharges on the Genoese who fell into a state of disorder when they heard the roar.' The English had first used what they called *crakys of war* against the

A medieval battle re-enactment.

Scots in 1327, and six years later Edward III had *gounes* at the siege of Berwick. Initially, both guns and powder were imported though both were soon being manufactured in England: the earliest Chamber and Issue Rolls show royal purchases of sulphur and saltpetre in 1333. Both substances continued to be bought in ever greater quantities to be made into gunpowder at the Tower of London. In 1345 Edward ordered the casting of *ribaldi*, or small cannon, before he sailed for France and it may have been these that were used at Crécy, mainly to frighten the enemy. They were certainly used later at the siege of Calais, and by the end of Edward's reign Froissart records that the English had as many as a hundred cannon and mortars at the siege of St Malo. As siege weapons, however, the guns available to Edward were still more for show than effect.[3]

You can train as a knight, if you're young, male and wealthy enough to afford the warhorse, as well as a riding horse or two, a packhorse, an esquire, a quality sword, lance and other assorted weaponry and, in the later fifteenth century, an exceedingly expensive suit of plate armour. You'll need to persuade a lord to take you into his household as a page. Then, as you learn the rudiments of horsemanship, swordsmanship, martial strategy and tactics and even courtesy and manners, you can progress to serving as an esquire to a knight. An esquire is a posh servant and you'll learn to care for the horses, polish your knight's armour and keep his weapons sharp, as well as mundane chores like serving his meals, helping him dress and getting him and his horse ready for war.

Finally, when all aspects are second nature to you, and if you've shown courage or exceptional prowess in the field of battle, your lord or, if you're lucky, the king himself, may see fit to dub you a knight bachelor. This is the lower rank of knighthood, but means you'll have your own esquire to serve you, though you'll have to help train him in return. If you excel as a knight, the king may create you a knight banneret with your own little flag – a banneret – to which lesser knights must rally in battle, following you as their captain. This is as high as a common fellow can go in the ranks and requires money, years of training and a lord's patronage, so isn't easy to achieve. My advice is to leave warfare to those who are trained for it from childhood, if you possibly can. It's a noisy, bloody, dirty business.

Studying the art of war

If you're serious about getting involved I would advise you to read the most popular instruction book of the day: Vegetius' hand book for soldiers, *De Re Militari,* [About Military Things]. Surprisingly, Publius Flavius Vegetius Renatus had written his book way back in the fourth century AD and no one had bettered it since. Vegetius wasn't even a soldier but more of a financial manager to the emperor, so perhaps his idea was that the emperor should be advised how best to spend his money on military matters and not waste it. What he wrote became the single most influential military treatise in the Western world, affecting European battle tactics, methods of warfare and military training right through the medieval period and beyond. Since anyone likely to wage war across Europe has probably read it, you'll be at a disadvantage if you don't. We know King Richard III had a copy.

Luckily, in 1408 Thomas, Lord Berkeley, translated the Latin version of Vegetius' book into English and at some point the text was updated to include the more modern weaponry becoming available, such as longbows and cannon. *De Re Militari* is divided into four sections.

The first is about selecting and training your men and covers daily exercise to keep them fit: running and jumping, marching and even swimming. How to handle swords, shields and other hand weapons is included with instructions for leaping on and off a horse with a sword in your hand. There are details on setting up and fortifying a camp depending on whether it's a hasty affair with the enemy close, or a more leisurely affair with time to spend on making it more defensible and comfortable.

The second book tells of the structure of Roman legions in Vegetius' day, which is interesting but not so relevant, but also includes a list of 'engines of war', added to by later writers to include new technologies such as gunpowder. Book three is more useful and well thumbed, setting out the general rules of warfare and the basics of military theory, including strategy, tactics and – most importantly – how to keep your army healthy and battle-ready. Here are a few vital points from Vegetius:

1. He who wants peace should prepare war.
2. The best plans are those of which the enemy knows nothing until they happen.
3. Every army should be kept busy and so remain sharp; idleness makes them dull.
4. Exercise and weapons practice keeps men more healthy than doctors and medicines.
5. Good commanders never fight openly in the field unless forced to do so by circumstance or unexpected happenings.[4]

The final book deals with the detailed construction of fortifications and the best ways to undermine and bring them down. There is also a section on naval warfare, shipbuilding and how best to foretell and cope with bad weather at sea.

Even if you don't have your own army to command, by studying Vegetius you will at least know what your leaders are doing wrong. However, don't be too free with your superior knowledge and excellent military advice; it could be dangerous. Kings, princes, dukes and lords always think they know best and, of course, God is on *their* side. Telling them they're making a big mistake could be your biggest mistake: they won't appreciate it and the consequences for you could be unpleasant, though whether that's any worse than defeat is hard to know beforehand. Perhaps you could just leave your copy of Vegetius lying around where they're certain to see it, book-marked to the relevant pages. If they do lose the battle, but you both survive, it's best not to say 'I told you so'.

What are my chances of survival?

If it happens that your local lord summons his tenants to fight for him, or the mayor calls the townsfolk to take up arms to defend the place, you'll want to know your chances of survival. There is both good and bad news. Medieval warfare is mostly a case of hand-to-hand combat. If you can dodge your immediate opponent's sword, pike or battleaxe, you stand a good chance. Remember though, he will be doing the same, trying to avoid your weapon, and if you succeed in knocking him down, there'll likely be another opponent behind him. Battle is a tiring business.

There are also the medieval equivalents of weapons of mass destruction coming into play. Firstly, the longbow with thousands of arrows shot at once by massed archers and the next wave of deadly arrowheads following just five seconds later. Whether accurately aimed or not, with so many shafts falling on hundreds of soldiers, a great many are likely to hit a target, either horse or human. Secondly, cannon are being used increasingly. At first, they are more useful for scaring the horses, and men are also afraid of these fearsome, deafening things, shooting fire and lumps of lead into the air. Cannon aren't particularly accurate, but even if you're hit more by luck than judgement the result can be devastating and messy.

DID YOU KNOW?

The first English nobleman to be killed, indirectly, by a cannon was John Talbot, Earl of Shrewsbury. At the battle of Castillon, near Bordeaux in France, on 17 July 1453. Talbot's horse was fatally injured by a cannon shot and fell, trapping Talbot beneath him so the French quickly finished him off.

In 1460 James II, king of Scots, was besieging the English fortress of Roxburgh Castle. Having the very latest in siege guns, the king was eager to have a go with his new toys and determined to fire one of the cannons himself. Warning: never carry out the first test firing in person. Unfortunately, this particular cannon was faulty and exploded in his face, killing the king immediately. Despite the loss of their monarch, the Scots continued the siege, undeterred, taking the castle – so it's said – without the loss of another single Scottish life. The number of English casualties from the bombardment isn't recorded.[5]

At the battle of Bosworth on 22 August 1485, King Richard III's chief commander, John Howard, Duke of Norfolk, was killed early on in the fray by a cannonball. This tragic loss was the beginning of the end for the king's cause that day. Norfolk's son, Thomas, Earl of Surrey, was thought to have been close by and injured by the same cannonball but recovered.

As you will realise, even noblemen can be killed or wounded in war. But, as King Henry V told us earlier, quite serious injuries are not necessarily fatal. Of course, kings, princes and dukes will be attended by the best surgeons, but in an age when a mere scratch can become inflamed, turn septic and prove fatal, what chance does a lowly foot soldier have if he's wounded? The answer is not quite as depressing as you might think.

Back in 1996 a mass grave was discovered not far from the site of the battle of Towton in Yorkshire. Around fifty skeletons were recovered, all male between the ages of sixteen and fifty. Many had met a violent end and the bones were carbon-dated, showing they were likely the casualties of Towton in 1461. Skeleton 'Towton 16' had an incredible history. He was quite tall, strong, and in his late forties and had died of a puncture wound to the head. However, this wasn't his first battle, or his first encounter

Towton 16's facial reconstruction.

126

with a weapon of war. Towton 16 had previously suffered a major blade injury to his jaw, slashing through his face on the left side and deep enough to damage the bone, shearing off a piece of it and taking a tooth as well. A surgeon with remarkable skills had removed the broken sliver of bone and treated the injury, which then healed without any sign that it became infected. Towton 16 recovered well enough that he lived to fight another day, until his luck ran out.[6] There is no evidence that he was anything but one of the foot soldiers, being buried in an unmarked grave with his fallen comrades, and yet he had previously received the very best of medical attention with a successful outcome. So all is not lost if you are wounded in war.

How would I be treated as a veteran?

The sad answer to this is, probably, not very well. There are no social services, and nobody has any concept of PTSD or the old idea of shell-shock. If you're obviously disabled, having lost a limb or your eyesight, then you will receive sympathy and maybe the authorities' permission to beg on the streets. Otherwise, a handout of alms from a monastery or the parish church coffers are your only hope, if you haven't got a family to support you.

To receive aid, beggars must be 'deserving' and having lost your leg may not be reckoned sufficient to prevent you earning a living as, say, a potter, a scribe or a cobbler, or at some other job which requires sitting down. If you've lost an arm, there are ways of earning a living one-handed, delivering messages as a courier, or serving in a tavern or cookshop, for example. As we saw in Chapter 7, everyone is expected to work, if at all possible. Let's ask one veteran of the battles of Barnet and Tewkesbury – both fought in 1471 between the Houses of York and Lancaster – about his experiences since:

> Good fellow, you are a beggar here on London's streets. Tell us how you came to be in this situation and how you manage.
>
> Well, it's pleasant to know that somebody still thinks I'm a "good fellow". Most prefer not to think about me at all, as if I'm invisible. But since I've got all day, I'll tell you all you want to know in exchange for some bread and ale.

That seems fair. How were you wounded?

Well, I survived Barnet Field with no more than a few scratches. But King Edward of York – the fourth, that is – having won his victory against that traitorous Earl of Warwick, still had to defeat Queen Margaret of Anjou's Lancastrian henchmen in the West Country. So I tagged along with my bow, having nought better to do, and we faced them rascals down at a place called Tewkesbury. I did well enough until late on, in the hand-to-hand fighting, when I was suddenly facing this giant of a fellow: a Goliath, seven feet tall, if he was an inch, and twice as broad.

How tall?

Well, he was big, believe me: a lot bigger than me. I came off worst, not surprisingly, though I did get him with my poleaxe, a couple of prods finding their mark. And then he slashed my arm with his blade. It was such a shock, I can tell you, seeing my own hand, still holding the pole, lying on the ground at my feet. It didn't even hurt, not at first, but all that blood gushing and knowing it was mine ... And then the devil went for my knee as well. I don't recall much after that.

But you survived.

Aye, and sometimes I wonder why the surgeons went to so much trouble. I was a thatcher before: up and down ladders all day, ridging, coursing and fixing the gads ... it's a very skilled craft, I tell you. But look at me now! No good for anything, except sitting here, outside St Paul's, rattling my begging bowl – not that it rattles much with only a bent farthing and pebble in it. That's all I've got since dawn this morning and, so I've been told, the bishop wants me to go sit somewhere else. Doesn't like seeing me every time he goes into the cathedral. I suppose I remind him he ought to be more charitable.

That sounds harsh.

It is. And folk around here know me and one or two are more generous than most, occasionally buying me a decent meal or inviting me to share their dinner. If I have to go elsewhere, nobody will know me, will they? Then what? I'll starve: that's what. Speaking of which, you promised me food and drink, earlier ... a good wedge of cheese, a heel of bread, some cold meats, onions in vinegar and a slice of fruit tart would go down well.

I said bread and ale, not a royal feast.

You're a heartless rascal; bad as the bishop.[7]

Take heed in medieval times: you don't want to end up as a beggar on the street, not even a deserving one, so beware.

Chapter 10

Law and Order

Medieval England is no different from the twenty-first century: people misbehave, act in an antisocial manner and break the law. Crime is a fact of life, and violence, I'm sorry to say, is an everyday occurrence. In 1202 in Lincoln, with a population of just 5,000 souls, 114 murder trials were held. Domestic violence, up to a point, is even considered quite acceptable. A man is reckoned to have the right to keep his wife in order by physical means and to punish his children is his expected duty. That said, 'keeping the king's peace' is required by law, but what does that mean for you on your time-travelling adventure?

How would I behave as a citizen?

In the event of a crime, if you discover it first, whether a street mugging or a burglary – still known by the Anglo-Saxon *infangenthef,* or as 'hedge-breaking' – you are obliged to 'raise the hue and cry' by shouting, blowing a horn, banging on doors or clattering pots and pans; any means of rousing the neighbours and anyone within earshot. The idea is that everyone should give chase and apprehend the culprit, presuming they know his or her identity and can catch them. Only small children, the sick or the lame are excused from taking up the pursuit if they hear the cries of alarm. Otherwise, under a statute of 1275, they are considered to be aiding and abetting the criminal and could find themselves arrested. However, if someone raises the hue and cry unnecessarily, they have to pay a fine of sixpence.

Burglaries after curfew are frequent in London, despite this being a capital crime, carrying the death sentence. Shops are robbed of jewellery, cloth, shoes and blades – anything that might turn a profit when sold on – and private houses are burgled for items of value. Theft of all kinds goes on, just like today. In 1502 a man was arrested in Cornhill for being a 'bribour and steler of pypes and gutters of lede by means of cutting of theym by nyghtes time'.

Cheating at games is also a crime. In December 1375 in London, Stephen Lalleford, a smith, was sent to prison, charged by the Alderman of Aldgate Ward as a 'common gamester with dice and chequers,' having cheated William Brounyng out of the huge sum of £17. He was released on bail, awaiting the jury's verdict.[1] Unfortunately, the jurors' decision isn't recorded.

If you go out after dark, as a good citizen you will have to carry a burning torch to light your way. This is so the watchmen will not mistake you for a villain, sneaking about and up to no good.

How is the country policed?

In the countryside, law and order is preserved by the county sheriff as the king's representative, in conjunction with the local lords, each responsible for policing their own manor. Towns are usually more organised. London has two sheriffs, a number of magistrates – the Lord Mayor being the chief – a Coroner to look into unexpected deaths and each ward appoints a beadle who is answerable to the alderman of the ward and in charge of a couple of constables. The beadles of London take an oath before the Lord Mayor to be honest and vigilant, though their wages are small.

DID YOU KNOW?

Today, the Ward Beadles hold the oldest elected office in the city, although their duties are now largely ceremonial.

Described as the alderman's watchdog, the beadle is usually the brains behind crime prevention and detection, knowing the unsavoury characters in his ward, such as thieves, cheats and women of ill repute, and sending a list of them to the alderman who then has fifteen days to act on the intelligence – as in Stephen Lalleford's case. If the alderman fails to act, the beadle informs the mayor. If there is a fight with weapons or a riot in the ward the beadle must report it to a sheriff who will send sergeants to assist, though in lesser cases the beadle and his brawny constables deal with the situation. The beadle also draws up the rota for the watchmen, organises juries and sends out 'skawagers' to 'inspect nuisances' such as rubbish blocking the street. In 1489 skawagers were made specifically responsible for catching Londoners who threw rubbish into the Thames. London also has a 'marching watch' patrolling the streets at night in addition to the watchmen for each ward.

Most beadles seem to be honest fellows; at least the records contain few complaints against them. However, there was a case in 1388 when a beadle was arrested and dismissed from office for telling lies about an alderman and a sheriff. This arrangement is the nearest medieval London has to a police force.

Unfortunately, even lesser crimes, like falling into debt, can end in a gaol sentence. Prostitution is a serious matter, made more so because brothels are reckoned to be the places where criminals get together to organise their activities and lay low after the event. For this reason, London has banned brothels, or 'stews', to the south side of the bridge, in Southwark. Southwark is regarded as a nest of sin, despite the fact that many churchmen have their town houses there. The Bishop of Winchester even rents out his Southwark properties to known brothel-keepers, leading to their employees – those women of loose morals – becoming known as 'Winchester geese'. Brothel-keepers are severely punished. For a first offence, a man has his hair and beard shaved off (for a woman, her hair is cut short) and taken to the pillory with minstrels playing for as long as the mayor orders. A second offence means imprisonment and a third results in banishment from the city.

The anonymous *London Lickpenny* poem of 1420 tells of the experiences of a country lad from Kent who comes to the city hoping to bring a law suit. Sadly, he has no money to pay a lawyer, so his journey is wasted. Instead, he suffers at the hands of street thieves, as in these excerpts:

Stanza 2

And as I thrust the press among,
By froward chance my hood was gone,
Yet for all that I stayed not long
Till to the King's Bench I was come.

Stanza 13

Then into Cornhill anon I yode,   [the past tense
of 'go' = went]

Where was much stolen gear among;
I saw where hung mine owne hood
That I had lost among the throng:
To buy my own hood I thought it wrong;
I knew it well as I did my Creed,
But for lack of Money I could not speed. [proceed]

Among the beadles' duties is investigating immorality. In 1474 the beadle of the ward of Farringdon Without suspected that Joan Salman and Walter Haydon, neither of them wedded, were alone together in a house near the Old Bailey. With two burly neighbours acting as constables, the beadle approached the house. It seems the door wasn't locked or barred from inside so the beadle and one of the neighbours went in, leaving the other neighbour at the door to prevent the couple making their escape. The two men crept quietly up the stairs to the bedchamber and caught Walter in bed with Joan – 'a loose, immoral woman' – there beside him. The pair were arrested and taken to the Counter (the sheriffs' prison). All in a day's work for the beadle.

The piepowder courts

With so many ways for tradesmen to cheat the customer, England has special courts, the piepowder courts, to deal swiftly with any crimes committed on the occasion of a fair or market. These courts have unlimited jurisdiction over events taking place in the market, including disputes between merchants, theft and acts of violence. Every town or village has its own piepowder court for the duration of the fair or market and cases must be heard on the spot and judgement passed on the same day, before tradesmen and customers go home.

London holds its piepowder court before the mayor, sheriffs and two or three aldermen. Punishments include fines and the possibility of being put in the pillory to humiliate the offender. More serious crimes are often reserved for the royal justices, but sometimes the jurisdiction is still held by the piepowder court. At the trial, both parties appear and the burden of proof is on the plaintiff, with documents and witnesses being called as evidence. After the plaintiff makes his case, the defendant has the right to respond to the accusation and counter with evidence of his own. This method of proof is quite advanced for the time compared to other courts. If the court rules against the defendant and the defendant can't pay the fine, his property may be seized, appraised and sold to cover the costs. Courts of piepowder exist because speedy justice is needed when people aren't permanent residents of the place where the market is held. In the case of London, few records remain of the court and later cases go to the more time-consuming mayor's and sheriffs' courts.

'Piepowder' originally referred to the dusty feet (in French, *pieds poudrés*) of travellers and is applied to the courts that had dealings with such people. Also, since the judges aren't sitting on a bench, but walking around the fair or market, they too have dusty feet.

Surprisingly, private enterprise is considered selfish. There is a medieval principle that too much profit is immoral. Craftsmen and merchants ought to be happy with a reasonable profit and not take advantage of their neighbours in need. There is even the 'scot and lot' regulation, which requires that anyone who gets a real bargain is obliged to share it with others, letting them buy the surplus from him at the same excellent price, keeping only a 'fair portion' for himself.

How are criminals prosecuted?

In medieval England the law sometimes works quite differently from the way we expect today. In 1249 a gang of thieves was terrorising Winchester, Salisbury and Guildford, specialising in stealing expensive clothing and shoes. The gang was often violent and though folk in the area knew who they were, they were too scared to accuse them. Let's speak to Walter Blowberme, a gang member:

> Now Walter, you were caught in the act, I believe, and admitted your crimes. Tell us what you did.
>
> Well, see, we stoled all this valuable stuff, didn't we? Good cloth, shoes, some jewellery and silver cups. Made a fine profit 'til I got caught, filching a gold brooch. I knewed this meant a date wi' the hangman for me so I told the sheriff I'd be an approver.

What is an approver?

You don't know? What a dim-wit. It means my life'll be spared if I telled the court the names of ten others involved in the crimes. I didn't want t' do it, 'cos they was my mates but a man has t' lookout for hisself.

So you snitched on your fellows. What happened then?

I named six fellows from Guildford who was all members of the gang. They was all arrested, tried and condemned. I didn't feel too bad about them 'cos I never liked most of 'em, except Tom. It was a shame about him. But I still needed another four fellows convicted to save my own neck, so I accused three from Hampshire. They wasn't in the gang; just fellows I knowed and didn't like much. They was found not guilty and released so I had t' name four others as gang members. It's a good thing I know so many folk and don't like none of 'em. These four was nasty bits o' work, I can tell you, but when the sheriff tried to take 'em, three managed to escape. But because they never turned up in court, they was found guilty anyway. The fourth fellow, Hamo Stare – my sister's husband what I never liked – was brung to trial but things was so complicated, the judge offered Hamo a trial by ordeal.

I thought trial by ordeal was made illegal by the Church?

Don't ask me; I'm not the judge. Anyhow, Hamo chosed trial by combat and I, as his accuser, had to be his opponent. We had wooden clubs and shields and fighted 'til we was both bloody but Hamo gave in first. The judge declared God had gived me most strength, so I must have spoke truly against Hamo. Hamo was hanged – good riddance – and I'd managed to get ten fellows convicted, so my life was spared but I got banished from the district forever 'cos I admitted being guilty of so many crimes.

But you didn't mend your ways, Walter?

Nay. Couldn't resist some silver bits, could I? I comed t' London and just six months later I got caught, thieving a chalice and candlesticks from St Mary-le-Bow church.

And this time there is no second chance for you, is there, Walter?

Nay. This time it's the gallows for me. T'morrow. Pray for me soul, won't you?[2]

Judicial tests and ordeals had been abolished at that important Lateran Council meeting in 1215, stating that churchmen may 'neither pronounce nor execute a sentence of death. Nor may they act as judges in extreme criminal cases, or take part in matters connected with'. This meant trial by ordeal no longer had God's sanction – a priest had to be present as His representative – since it was God who determined the outcome. Obviously, however, such trials continued over thirty years later.

Church men cannot sit in judgement, but neither can they be tried in a state court. Only church courts can try clerics and can never pass a death sentence, even for murder. So, if you can prove you're a man of the cloth, or a nun, then you can, literally, get away with murder. Here's how: only trained clerics can read Latin; so if the accused can read the Bible – always in Latin – he must be a churchman. To prove you can read, the same passage is always required to be read aloud from the Bible: 'Oh loving and kind God, have mercy. Have pity upon my transgressions' (Psalm 51, Verse 1).

Walter (left) fighting Hamo (right) and Hamo being hanged after he lost.

Top tip

Learn this 'Neck-Verse' by heart, in Latin. It's saved the necks of many criminals who learned it by heart even if they could not read. It could get you out of trouble.

For common folk arrested in London, there is every chance they'll be remanded in one of the city's many prisons: the Fleet, the King's Bench, Ludgate or the Tower (for more important political prisoners), or the Clink or the Marshalsea across the Thames in Southwark. All are dreadful places where the inmates are as likely to die at the hand of a fellow prisoner or of disease before coming to trial as of execution afterwards.

Perhaps the worst outcome for anyone arrested is to be remanded to Newgate Gaol in London. The first mention of prisoners in Newgate dates to 1218. Dick Whittington left a bequest in his will to pay for the infamous hell-hole to be rebuilt in 1423. The fine new gaol was jokingly called 'Whittington's Palace', a title soon reduced to 'the Whit' as the place descended into an abysmal state every bit as terrible as its forebear.

The prison is managed by the two annually elected sheriffs who, in turn, hand over the running of Newgate to private gaolers (or keepers) for a price. The keepers make a handsome profit by exacting payment directly from the inmates, so the position is one of the most lucrative in London. The keepers can be very cruel, charging the prisoners for everything from entering the gaol to having their chains put on and taken off. Among the most notorious keepers were the fourteenth-century gaolers Edmund Lorimer, who was infamous for charging inmates four times the legal limit for the removal of irons, and Hugh de Croydon, who was eventually convicted of blackmailing prisoners in his care.

Out on bail

While imprisoned a person's property is unprotected. If found innocent and released after trial, they might discover their property has been confiscated or their house rented out to someone else. All this is quite legal, so King Richard III, in his Parliament of January 1484, introduced the possibility of bail for those accused of non-capital crimes so their property can't be taken over in their absence. King Richard III isn't everyone's favourite monarch, but in the single Parliament of his short two-year reign, assembled on the 23 January 1484, a number of statutes were passed that clearly show his progressive and liberal attitude towards law and order.

One ploy being used by lords who covet their neighbour's prime piece of land is to have the neighbour arrested and imprisoned on a trumped-up charge, and in his absence shift the boundary fences to include the land desired. Then, even when the neighbour is found innocent and released, it will take an expensive court case for him to prove that land is really his; if he can afford a good lawyer. Otherwise, possession, as they say, is nine-tenths of the law and the lord has got what he wanted. Bail protected suspects from imprisonment before trial.

The idea of 'bail' had existed for centuries but Richard's Parliament set the law down in such a form that it applied to lords and labourers alike:

> Because various people are arrested and imprisoned daily on suspicion of felony, sometimes out of malice and sometimes on vague suspicion, and thus kept in prison without bail […] to their great vexation and trouble; be it therefore ordained […] that no sheriff or bailiff or any other person shall seize the goods of any person arrested on suspicion of felony before the person has been convicted or attainted of the felony according to the law. Upon pain of forfeiting double the value of the goods thus taken to the person harmed in that respect.[3]

Forest law

In the twenty-first century we think of a forest as a place full of trees but in medieval England 'forest' meant an area reserved for royal hunting. A forest could include entire villages and parishes, as well as woodlands, marshes and heathland (See Chapter 1). William the Conqueror was so keen on hunting that he created the New Forest in

Hampshire in 1079 with special Forest laws to protect the 'venison and vert': the beasts of the chase and the greenery they depended upon.

Depending on when and where you arrive in medieval England, these harsh laws may be enforced by the king's verdurers; literally wardens caring for the greenery. Common folk aren't allowed to hunt in the forest, even for a rabbit or pigeon for the pot, and their dogs are required to have parts of their paws amputated or 'expedited' so they cannot chase after game. However, the verdurers can only legally arrest you in four situations, so make sure you understand these:

1. Stable stand. That is, found with a long-bow or cross-bow bent at the ready or with dogs on a leash ready to let them off.
2. Dog draw. That is, discovered with a wounded deer or wild boar or found using a dog to follow its scent in order to catch it.
3. Back bear. That is, carrying away a slain animal on your back.
4. Bloody hand. That is, being caught in the forest 'red handed' with your hands covered in blood.

Caught in any of these situations, you can be arrested and imprisoned to await trial at one of a complicated system of courts, depending on the seriousness of your alleged crime. The Court of Attachment is held every forty days and presided over by verdurers and the warden. This court deals with the hearing and doesn't have the power to try or convict. If the case is serious enough, it passes on to the more senior Swainmote. This court tries offenders before a jury of freemen and is held three times a year. Cases of persistent poaching and further offences committed can be brought before the highest-ranking Court of Justice Eyre, which is only held every three years or more. This could mean a long spell in prison awaiting trial, unless it's after 1484 and you can get bail. Otherwise, you may not survive to meet the judge. You have been warned.

Oddities of the law

After reading one of my novels recently, a reader contacted me to tell me my medieval character would not have been hanged, drawn and quartered for having committed murder since this horrific punishment was reserved solely for the crime of treason. The reader was correct up to a point, but the medieval definition of treason was then much wider.

In medieval England treason isn't only a crime perpetrated against the king or the state; it includes any kind of serious rebellion that upsets the law and what is seen as the 'natural' order of things as God has created them. Forging coins corrupts the country's financial system, so that counts as treason. The punishment for the crime of 'petty' treason is the same as for treason proper and such law-breaking includes the killing of a husband by his wife – but not vice versa – of a lord by his servant, of an ecclesiastic by a subordinate or a layman, or, as in my novel, the murder of a master by his journeyman or apprentice. It also includes having knowledge of someone plotting to commit treason but not informing the authorities of their heinous plans. For anyone found guilty of petty treason, it can be the full penalty inflicted, as described, or some lesser degree, if there are reasons for clemency. If a woman is found guilty of petty treason, perhaps for killing her abusive husband, she may be condemned to suffer burning at the stake, though this is usually commuted to hanging which is thought to be a kinder death.

However, any woman thus condemned may claim to be pregnant – midwives are brought in to check this out if it isn't obvious – and sentence is delayed until after the birth, if she's telling the truth, so the innocent babe doesn't suffer for its mother's crime. Unsurprisingly, rather a lot of women use this as a reason to put off the inevitable and it's known that seducing the gaoler in the hope of getting pregnant does happen.

In 1316 Juliana Gayton was accused of having persuaded her servants to kill her husband and was arrested. She seems to have used her feminine charms, firstly on the Sheriff of Staffordshire, and then on the Sheriff of Warwickshire. She avoided no fewer than five appearances at the Court of King's Bench in London by claiming she was pregnant. Not until 1321 was she finally tried, found guilty of petty treason and sentenced to be burned, though this was commuted to hanging at the last minute.

Other women had their ruse discovered. On a September day in the fourteenth century (year not given), Elizabeth Taillour and Alice Rolff, both silkwomen of London, attacked a rival, Elizabeth Knollys. They grabbed Knollys and drowned her in a wash tub. Trying to conceal the crime, they then burned the body and threw the remains into a latrine pit. Not until November was the corpse discovered and the truth revealed. Taillour confessed and was sentenced to hang, but Rolff said she was pregnant. However, a jury of midwives determined that Rolff was lying about her condition and she hanged with her partner in crime.[4]

If all else fails, there is the possibility of claiming sanctuary in a church. The Eyre Roll for Kent records that in 1314 a pregnant woman condemned for larceny (theft of personal property) was kept in prison to await the baby's birth, but managed to escape and sought sanctuary in a church nearby. Unlawfully, the gaoler dragged her out and took her before the justices. They decided she should be allowed her forty days of sanctuary in the church and then be forced to 'abjure the realm'; i.e., be banished from England. The gaoler was tried for having broken her right to sanctuary.[5]

A more unusual case was recorded by the Sussex coroner in July 1490. Let's ask him what happened in this case:

Good Sir Coroner, can you tell us about this recent and most unusual case?

What business is it of yours?

We are interested is all. Curious.

Nosey, you mean. Ah, well, I suppose ... The case concerned Margaret, wife of Ralph Derbye, a labourer, on her way to Petworth market. She was riding her husband's grey mare and was in a hurry when, in Shopton Lane in Sutton, she found the king's highway blocked by a cart belonging to John Brownyng, a yeoman. Not wanting to waste time, waiting for the cart to be moved, Margaret threw caution to one side and forced the mare to climb a four-foot high embankment, in order to pass by the cart. But the embankment was too steep. Margaret slipped from the mare's back, fell to the ground on her neck, receiving a large wound on the neck of which she immediately died.

Sounds like an unfortunate accident to me: what you coroners call a case of "misadventure" wasn't it?

Which just shows how ignorant you are. It wasn't a case of misadventure at all. The mare was guilty of murdering her!

But the horse could hardly have intended to kill Margaret. Can a dumb animal be guilty of malice aforethought? Isn't that what makes a crime of murder?

Be silent. My verdicts are final – always, you impertinent jackanapes.

So, did the poor horse have to stand trial?

The verdict of my inquest was sufficient. The mare is yet deodand.

Whatever does that mean, Sir Coroner?

It means the horse is forfeit to the king, if he ever has a use for it. However, since the wretched beast is worth no more than five shillings, I cannot imagine the king will ever want it, so, for the time being, it remains with Ralph Derbye. Thus he has to feed it and care for it, all the while reserving it for the king's use.

At least you didn't hang the poor thing. Good day to you, Sir Coroner.[6]

Although this guidebook is concerned with medieval England, you may wish to travel overseas during your visit. Therefore, it is as well to be aware of some oddities concerning crime and punishment in France. These cases are difficult to take seriously in the twenty-first century, but they were of great concern at the time. The French seem to be even more especially keen to prosecute animals than the English. Pigs are given a particularly hard time, but lesser creatures are not let off lightly either, as in these three cases.

In 1386, in Falaise in Normandy, a pig was accused of murdering an infant. She was tried and convicted by a court and hanged at the gallows by the village hangman. Her six piglets were charged with being accessories to the crime but were acquitted 'on account of their youth and their mother's bad example'.

The Grand Vicar of Valence, who must surely have been quite mad, brought a case against some caterpillars. They were accused of wilfully destroying his crops and summoned to appear in court. When the malefactors didn't appear to defend themselves, a lawyer was appointed for them. However, he failed to make an adequate case for the caterpillars and the court found them guilty as charged and banished them from the diocese. No doubt they complied, eventually, turning into innocent butterflies and flying away from that mad place.

A pig stands trial for murder.

Finally, the rats of Autun in France had a gifted lawyer to defend them. The rats were accused by the local barley growers of thieving their grain. The lawyer, Chassenee, claimed that the case could only proceed if every rat in the diocese was summoned to court so that those that were guilty – if any were – could be divided from the innocent rodents. So all rats were duly ordered to appear. Non-appearance was usually taken as an admission of guilt but when the rats didn't come to court, clever Chassenee argued that every felon was deserving of safe conduct to and from the trial. Since the rats couldn't be certain of not being eaten by the local cats on their journey, they were too afraid to appear. The rats were therefore acquitted in their absence and Chassenee became the lawyer of choice for all local felons, two-legged, four-legged or winged.

Conclusion

That ends my guide to surviving in Medieval England. I hope I've answered many of your most pressing questions and you now have the basic information needed in order to blend in with the locals during your adventure back in time to the Middle Ages.

I can't stress enough that your good health will probably depend on you having had all the injections necessary for a visit to a Third World country before you go, as well as full health and dental check-ups.

Think of it as a voyage of exploration and discovery to unknown regions, although the landscape may seem somewhat familiar. Leave your electronic gadgets behind; they'll be no use to you as you can't recharge them and there'll be no wi-fi or SatNav signals.

Expect dirt, discomfort and hard work, along with language difficulties, at least to start with. I'm sure you'll soon adapt to all these changes and get used to the sound and meanings of Chaucer's Middle English. You will be experiencing history, first-hand; something no one has ever done before.

When you return, you can rewrite this book, adding all the extra advice you have acquired and correcting any errors I've made, and omitting information you found unnecessary. Obviously I haven't been there, so this is only an armchair-traveller's guide. Even so, I hope you find it helpful.

I wish you good luck on your time-travelling adventure and a safe return to your home century, whenever that is. Enjoy!

P.S. In case of emergencies, don't forget to learn the 'Neck Verse' in Latin.

Notes

Chapter 1: Introduction

1. Possibly, you'll have hundreds of great-great... etc.-grandparents alive, each of whom survived long enough to produce at least one child who also survived long enough to produce at least one child, and so on. In theory, if you travel back to 1215, the year King John signed the Magna Carta, four out of every five people you meet will be your forebears. The only reason that doesn't work out in fact is because the population is so small, for many generations people have to marry their cousins and second cousins, reducing the total number of grandparents involved every time this happens.

Chapter 2: Social Structure and Housing

1. H. S. Bennett, *Life on an English Manor,* (Cambridge University Press, 1937, pp61-62).
2. Fictionalised interview using factual material from Margaret Wade Labarge, *Life in a Baronial Household of the Thirteenth Century,* (Phoenix Paperback, 2003).
3. Will of Ellen Langwith, fols.9-11v transcribed by the author in L. Boatwright, M. Habberjam & P. Hammond [eds], *The Logge Register of Prerogative Court of Canterbury Wills, 1479-86,* (Richard III Society, 2008).

Chapter 3: Beliefs and Religious Ideas

1. P.J.P. Goldberg, *Women in England, c.1275-1525,* (Manchester University Press, 1995, p262, No. 5).

2. Adapted from Maggie Black, *The Medieval Cookbook,* (British Museum Press, 1992, pp63-64).
3. P.J.P. Goldberg, *Women in England, c.1275-1525,* (Manchester University Press, 1995, p271, [b]).
4. Fictionalised interview using factual material from 'Three Fifteenth-Century Vowesses' by Mary C. Erler in *Medieval London Widows, 1300-1500,* edited by Caroline M. Barron & Anne F. Sutton (The Hambledon Press, 1994, pp171-75).

Chapter 4: Clothing and Appearance

1. See The National Archives [TNA] MS E101 for details of Sumptuary Laws.
2. Statute of Apparel, 1463.
3. Ruth Goodman, *How to be a Tudor,* (Penguin, 2015, pp23-24).
4. University of Innsbruck http://www.uibk.ac/urgeschichte/projekte_forschung/textilien-lengberg/medieval-lingerie-from-lengberg-castle-east-tyrol.html

Chapter 5: Food and Shopping

1. Blaunderelles are described as white apples, good for the digestion. Chibols are a type of little onion not unlike salad onions or spring onions. Lampreys are tiny, eel-like fish. King Henry I is said to have died of eating 'a surfeit of lampreys' or – more likely – food-poisoning.
2. Adapted from Maggie Black, *The Medieval Cookbook* (British Museum Press, 1992, pp5-47).
3. Fictionalised interview using factual material from Lorna J. Sass, *To the King's Taste* (Metropolitan Museum of Art, New York, 1975, pp11-20).
4. *Calendar of Plea & Memoranda Rolls of the City of London* (Cambridge University Press, 1929, p66).
5. *Calendar of Plea & Memoranda Rolls of the City of London* (Cambridge University Press, 1929, p180).
6. Molly Harrison, *People and Shopping* (Ernest Benn Ltd, 1975, p24).

Chapter 6: Health and Medicine

1. From *Reliquiae Antiquae,* a fourteenth century fragment of manuscript, (Thomas Wright [ed] 1841).
2. P.W. Hammond & Anne F. Sutton, *Richard III – The Road to Bosworth Field* (Constable & Co., 1985, p23).
3. Fictionalised interview using factual material from J. K. Mustain, 'John Crophill – A Rural Medical Practitioner in Fifteenth-Century England' in *Bulletin of the History of Medicine* 46 (1972, pp473-74).
4. C. H. Talbot & E. A. Hammond, *The Medical Practitioners of Medieval England – A Biographical Register* (Wellcome Historical Medical Library, London, 1965, p241).
5. More information on both Richard Esty and William Hobbys can be found in Toni Mount, *Medieval Medicine – Its Mysteries & Science* (Amberley, 2015, pp43-44, 66-69, 164-65, 103, 181 & 197). Richard Esty's medical handbook (1454) was the subject of the author's thesis for her MA by Research (unpublished but available at the Wellcome Library for the History of Medicine, London, 2009).

Chapter 7: Work and Leisure

1. Caroline M. Barron, 'Johanna Hill and Johanna Sturdy, Bell-Founders' in [Caroline M. Barron & Anne F. Sutton [eds], *Medieval London Widows, 1300-1500* (The Hambledon Press, 1994, pp99-111).
2. Toni Mount, *Medieval Housewives and Women of the Middle-Ages* (Echoes from History, 2007, p31).
3. Fictionalised interview using factual material from various sources including the Catalogue for the V & A's *English Medieval Embroidery, Opus Anglicanum* exhibition, (London, 2016-17, p43); Caroline M. Barron, *London in the Later Middle Ages,* (Oxford UP, 2004, pp324-27); Sylvia L. Thrupp, *The Merchant Class of Medieval London,* (Ann Arbor, 1962, p327); John O'Connell, *The Book of Spice,* (Profile Books, 2015, pp230-33).
4. Caroline M. Barron, 'Medieval Queens of Industry' in *BBC History Magazine,* (June 2014, p32).

Chapter 8: Family Matters

1. The author's modern translation of 'How The Wise Man Taught His Son', stanza 12 in John Russell's *Babees Boke of Nurture* (British Library, Harley MS.2399 and five other manuscript versions).
2. P. J. P. Goldberg, *Women in England, c.1275-1525,* (Manchester UP, 1995, p118 [d]).
3. B. A. Hanawalt, *Growing Up in Medieval London: The Experience of Childhood in History,* (Oxford UP, 1993, pp217-22).
4. Fictionalised interview using factual material from Marie Barnfield, 'Diriment Impediments, Dispensations and Divorce: Richard III and Matrimony', a paper in *The Ricardian,* (The Richard III Society, 2007, pp84-98).
5. P. J. P. Goldberg, *Women in England, c.1275-1525,* (Manchester UP, 1995, pp219-21, No. 17).
6. Shannon McSheffrey, *Marriage, Sex and Civic Culture in Late Medieval London,* (Pennsylvania UP, 2006, pp166-67).
7. R. Virgoe, *The Illustrated Letters of the Paston Family,* (Macmillan, 1989, p183).
8. H. S. Bennett, *The Pastons and their England,* (Cambridge UP, 1990, pp45-46).
9. This painting, created c.1490, is in the National Museum in Kracow, Poland.

Chapter 9: Warfare

1. Fictionalised interview using factual material from Toni Mount, *Warrior Kings of England,* (MadeGlobal Medieval Courses Online, 2017, Module 10).
2. Toni Mount, *Warrior Kings of England,* (MadeGlobal Medieval Courses Online, 2017, Module 22).
3. Toni Mount, *Warrior Kings of England,* (MadeGlobal Medieval Courses Online, 2017, Module 17).
4. Paraphrased by the author from Anne F. Sutton & Livia Visser-Fuchs, *Richard III's Books* (Alan Sutton Publishing, 1997, pp77-80).

5. Asloan Manuscript, MS.16500, f.247 https://digital.nls.uk/scotland spages/timeline/1460.html
6. H. Miller, *Secrets of the Dead* (Macmillan, 2000, pp33-34).
7. Fictionalised interview using factual material from 'The Medieval Paupers' by L. H. Nelson, *Lectures Medieval History* http://www.vlib.us/medieval/lectures/paupers.html

Chapter 10: Law and Order

1. A. H. Thomas [ed.], *Calendar of Plea and Memoranda Rolls of the City of London, 1364-81* (Cambridge UP, 1929, p210).
2. Fictionalised interview using factual material from The National Archives [TNA], Hampshire Plea Roll, KB 26/223 (date: 1249).
3. C. Given-Wilson et al., [eds.] *The Parliament Rolls of Medieval England,* https://www.british-history.ac.uk/no-series/parliament-rolls-medieval
4. B. Holsinger, 'Sin City: thievery, prostitution and murder in medieval London' in *BBC History Magazine*, (February 2014).
5. P. J. P. Goldberg, *Women in England c.1275-1525,* (Manchester UP, 1995, pp238-39, No.33).
6. P. J. P. Goldberg, *Women in England c.1275-1525,* (Manchester UP, 1995, p171, No.4).

Credits for Illustrations

1 British Library, The Luttrell Psalter, 14th century, Add. MS 42130, f.171r, Public Domain

2 with kind permission of Peter Crossman of Crossman Crafts, pic GRM

3 Li Livres dou Santé (13th century), MS Sloane 2435, f.85, British Library/Bridgeman Art Library, Public Domain

4 Peter O'Connor, aka anemoneprojectors, Wikipedia Creative Commons

5 Andrew Fogg, Wikipedia Creative Commons

6 Weald & Downland Museum, Sussex, pic GRM

7 British Library, The De Lisle Psalter, 14th century, Arundel MS 83, f.127r, Public Domain

8 Ss Peter's and Paul's Church, Pickering, Yorks, Wikipedia Creative Commons

9 Bibliothèque de l'Arsenal, Paris Book of Regnault de Montauban 1300-20 (MS Arsenal 5073)

10 Institute of Archaeology, University of Innsbruck

11 Tacuinum Sanitatis, Northern Italy, 14th century, Österreichische Nationalbibliothek, Vienna, Codex Vindobonensis S.N. 2644, Wikipedia Creative Commons

12 Leeds Castle, Kent, pic GRM

13 Weald & Downland Museum, Sussex, pic GRM

14 British Library, The Luttrell Psalter, 14th century, Add. MS 42130, f.207v

15 Mondo senza fine le prime immagini 04 48227, Public Domain

16 pic GRM

17 British Library, Add MS 89066 1, f.61v

18 British Library, Add MS 47682, f.31

19 British Library, Royal MS 10 E IV, f.58

20   British Library, Landsdown MS 451, f.230

21   British Library, Royal MS 10 E IV, f. 29v

22   British Library, English Book of Hours, 13th century, Harley MS 928, f. 44v

23   British Library, The Luttrell Psalter, 14th century, Add MS 42130, f.147v

24   pic Pat Patrick c Owl & Trig Pillar (Blandford)

25   Malinn Hulst, Granada Television

26   Trial by combat from an assize roll from the reign of Henry III (1216-1272), Library of Congress blog https://blogs.loc.gov/law/2018/09/judicial-combat-barbarous-relic-or-timeless-litigation-strategy/

27   'Trial of a sow and pigs at Lavegny, 1457', The Book of Days: a miscellany of popular antiquities by Robert Chambers 1869, Wikipedia Creative Commons

Suggested Further Reading

Black, M., *The Medieval Cookbook,* (British Museum Press, 1992).

Goodman, R., *How to be a Tudor,* (Penguin, 2015).

Hardy, R., *Longbow – A Social and Military History,* (Sutton Publishing, 2006).

Hartnell, J., *Medieval Bodies*, (Wellcome Collection, 2019).

Jones, D., *The Plantagenets,* (William Collins, 2012).

Jones, T., *Medieval Lives,* (BBC Books, 2004).

Mount, T., *Everyday Life in Medieval London,* (Amberley, 2014).

Mount, T., *Medieval Housewives & Other Women of the Middle Ages,* (Amberley, 2014).

Mount, T., *Medieval Medicine – Its Mysteries and Science,* (Amberley, 2016).

Oledzka, E., *Medieval & Renaissance Interiors,* (British Library, 2016).

Picard, L., *Chaucer's People,* (Weidenfeld & Nicolson, 2017).

Sass, L.J., *To the King's Taste,* (Metropolitan Museum of Art, N.Y., 1975).

Index